DRESSAGE Q & A
with Janet Foy

D1567763

ALSO BY JANET FOY

Dressage for the Not-So-Perfect Horse

DRESSAGE Q & A
with Janet Foy

◇◇◇◇◇◇◇◇◇◇◇◇◇◇◇◇◇◇◇◇◇◇

HUNDREDS OF YOUR
QUESTIONS ANSWERED:
HOW TO RIDE, TRAIN,
COMPETE — AND LOVE IT!

JANET FOY

TRAFALGAR SQUARE
North Pomfret, Vermont

First published in 2015 by
Trafalgar Square Books
North Pomfret, Vermont 05053

Library of Congress Cataloging-in-Publication Data

Foy, Janet.
 Dressage Q & A with Janet Foy : hundreds of your questions answered :
how to ride, train, compete, and love it! / Janet Foy.
    pages cm
 Includes index.
 ISBN 978-1-57076-674-9
1. Dressage. I. Title.
 SF309.5.F67 2015
 798.2'3--dc23
                                        2015013560

Illustrations by Nicole Cotton Ackerman
Cover design by RM Didier
Book design by Brian Prendergast (www.brianpgraphics.com)
Typeset in Adobe Raleigh and Adobe Myriad Pro
Printed in United States of America
10 9 8 7 6 5 4 3 2 1

Dedication

To all of my Facebook friends and clinic students who helpfully submitted questions and their "Aha! moments." May your journey with your best friend be an educational and fulfilling one. Happy Riding!

CONTENTS

Acknowledgments

I would like to thank all of the wonderful editors at Trafalgar Square Books for their help, guidance, and occasional reprimand! You helped make my journey easier!

INTRODUCTION

When the topic of this book was discussed, I thought it would be a great way to answer all the questions I have from my dressage friends. I have arranged it in two sections:

Part 1 deciphers much of what many call "dressage babble" into common sense we can all understand in a basic "glossary," and then later, you will find a chapter on how you, the rider, learn, as well as one on how your horse learns (see pp. 15 and 35). Questions can be found at the end of each of these chapters, too, and I do my best to clarify difficult and confusing issues in my answers.

All along I thought it would be best to organize the questions I've received along the lines of the dressage Training Pyramid. So in Part 2 I have shared my thoughts about each step of the Pyramid from *rhythm* to *collection,* beginning on page 49. This is helpful in several ways: First, it gives me a logical place to put each question and answer (Q & A), and second, it gives all of you a review of the stages of the Training Pyramid and why it is important that you follow this scale of training with your horse. I found it very interesting to see on which topic the majority of the questions I received were based. Not surprisingly, it was *contact!* I have always felt that this is the hardest part of dressage to teach because it is about "feel." Feel is hard to teach, and most people don't have it by nature, so it must be learned. During a lesson, think about how many times you hear, "Do you feel that?"

Following discussion of the Pyramid, you'll find chapters on movements and showing. Throughout, I often reference my first book *Dressage for the Not-So-Perfect Horse.* Please know this is because I go into great detail when it comes to how to actually perform movements in that book, an effort I do not repeat here.

It is my hope this book will help your dressage journey: the problems and solutions (Q & As) address often-asked questions about dressage, and the commonsense approaches I offer should make your learning easier and more fun. Lastly, by sharing many riders' "Aha!" moments in sidebars throughout, I hope you won't have to wait so long to have your own similar breakthroughs!

Commonsense Dressage

CHAPTER ONE

Dressage Terms Made Simple

I think a large part of the problem of educating dressage riders in the United States is the language. We are not a country with "horse" words. In German, there are many dressage words that take a whole sentence in English to explain. And, many of the terms that have been translated from German to English are confusing—with the English not properly describing what they mean. Often, I hear this called "dressage babble."

I think we need to speak in a more simple language. I am sure some of my dressage-word definitions will offend the highly educated in biomechanics, so please pardon my attempt to *not* get complicated. So with the theme of "let's keep it simple," here is my list of definitions, presented alphabetically, with a dash of common sense:

ACCURACY

Being *accurate* in the arena when riding figures is one of the most important—and frequently ignored—concepts in dressage. You need to learn to love geometry; know how many meters are between each letter; plot the figures you are riding on a graph. At all levels, the ability to ride accurate figures and completely use the corners of the arena will tell you a lot about the control you have over your horse. Don't lose "stupid" points for inaccuracy. Accuracy is perhaps the easiest dressage concept to practice at home, then improve at a show.

ACTIVITY

Activity refers to the bending of the horse's hind legs while they are in the air. An active hind leg will come up and down in the air and show good articulation of the joints. This type of hind leg may or may not help with *engagement* (see p. 8). Think of a Hackney.

AGAINST THE BIT

When the horse is *against the bit*, he pulls down or pushes into the bit by using his under-neck muscles or stiffening his poll. Visually, you will see the horse's under-neck muscles bulging.

AIDS

The rider has three *aids* in dressage: Your legs, your hands, and your seat. That's it. Simple.

BALANCE

Balance is an important term. It refers to the balance of the horse in relationship to the dressage levels. For Training and First Level, the horse should be carrying the *same* amount of weight on all four legs. In other words, this horse is in a *level balance*. In a level balance, his hind legs are pushing him forward over the ground. At Second Level, the balance should show a tendency to stay uphill. His hind legs now carry more weight than the front legs. Due to this "carrying" effect (called *engagement*), he will thrust up in the air before he moves forward over the ground. Think of a spring coiling and uncoiling. The balance requirement and the strength of the carrying power of the hind legs increases as the horse moves up the levels.

BASICS

The *basics* are made up from elements on the Training Pyramid. When your basics are correct, your horse can perform all three gaits in the correct rhythm. Correct basics improve the quality of the gaits: the horse will have a supple back and stretch elastically into an even contact, and you will have a forward-thinking horse. You will be able to ride him on the line of travel and with these elements in place, balance will improve toward *collection*.

BEHIND THE BIT

This term is often used incorrectly: it's not *just* the position of the head. The horse can be *behind the bit* with a long neck as well as a short neck. Behind the bit really means the horse drops contact or avoids contact with the bit—in both reins. Often, this horse is actually *behind the leg*. So, my definition is that the horse is resisting going forward from the rider's leg because he is not "over the back" and stretching into the contact. Tension,

either mental or physical, often plays a role here. Remember, a horse is not "light" or in self-carriage when he drops the contact. It is a major evasion.

BEHIND THE LEG

The horse that is *behind the leg* is ignoring the rider's inside leg and seat; the influence of the rider over the horse's hind legs is not correct. Behind the leg is not generally used to describe a tense horse; it usually means a horse that is deemed lazy, dull, or inattentive.

BEHIND THE VERTICAL

Here's a visual indicator to describe this: the horse's forehead is no longer perpendicular to the ground but instead, his nose has dipped closer to his chest. When *behind the vertical* he may or may not be "behind the leg" or "behind the bit" at the same time, and the poll may still be the highest point or the poll may be too low.

BEND

The term *bend* concerns the *entire* body of the horse. To keep it simple, think of your horse on a circle as being like a three-car "choo-choo" train: there are connections between the "cars" in front of the saddle and behind the saddle. In order for the horse to bend, the cars must conform to the line of travel—like a letter "C." The shoulder-and-neck "car" comes in, the rib cage (dining car) moves out, and the hind end (caboose) stays in, following the tracks on a circle or curve.

BENDING AIDS

These are the *lateral bending aids* that keep your choo-choo train (see above) on the line of travel. The *inside rein* bends the horse's head and neck and turns the shoulders. The *inside leg* at the girth pushes the dining car (rib cage) out, and the *outside leg* behind the girth keeps the caboose (hind end) from falling out. The *outside rein* tells the horse how much to bend the neck and keeps the neck attached to the shoulders, so the outside shoulder doesn't jump the track. Think of your train going around a curve and you will get the idea.

CADENCE

This word is used in collection and only in trot and canter, as *cadence* is about airtime (suspension) and the walk does not have this moment of suspension. *Rhythm* refers to the *footfalls* of the legs, while cadence refers to the *tempo* of the beat. In other words, a correct two-beat rhythm with a moment of suspension can have a varied tempo, either faster (as in piaffe, due to a *decreased* airtime) or slower (as in passage, the slowest tempo in trot) due to *increased* airtime. When a horse has a natural cadence, you see a longer period of suspension. Correct training and the gymnastic development of the horse increases the cadence or airtime of the gaits.

COLLECTION

When the horse has enough *collection* (balance) for the level of dressage in which he is competing, his movement will be effortless and he will not struggle with the figures or transitions.

CONTACT

Reins that are floppy cannot have a correct *contact*, nor can reins that are *non*-elastic or restrictive. Some horses like the contact to be a bit heavier, some a bit lighter. Regardless, you should have equal contact with both reins since both reins are a team—they work together. Approximately 2 to 5 pounds weight in each rein is fine. Contact should be elastic, and the weight will come and go, with the most weight being when the shoulders go downward in the canter, and the lightest contact when the shoulders are up in the air. Finding a way to keep a supple and elastic contact is the most difficult thing to learn (and teach) in dressage (see chapter 7, p. 79).

CROOKEDNESS

When the horse is *crooked*, the choo-choo train (see Bend, p. 6) has derailed and is no longer on the line of travel. For example, the caboose (hind end) is falling out in the corners, or perhaps, falling in on the long side. Horses also like to "push" their shoulder-and-neck "car" to the outside of the line of travel. When any of these "derailments" happen, the horse will lose balance and consequently engagement, too. Many riders lose the horses hindquarters in corners or turns. When I see this, I know the next movement (perhaps an extension) is going to have balance problems.

CROSS-CANTER

Cross-cantering means the horse is cantering on both leads at the same time—that is, cantering on one lead in front and the other in back. It often occurs because of tension in the back or resistance to the bending aids (he usually loses the lead behind due to tension in the back). Also, a rider who is sitting in the wrong direction on a straight line can cause a loss of the correct hind lead. By this, I mean that because the rider is no longer sitting on the horse's inside hind leg, her shift in weight causes the horse to lose balance, which results in cross-cantering. The loss of the hind lead is quite often seen at the end of the lengthening or medium canter. Losing the lead in front is usually a balance issue rather than a tension issue, and caused by the horse's shoulders falling out.

CURLED-UP

The horse's neck can do a lot of interesting things. I think that nature gave the neck to the horse as a balancing rod, much like a tightrope walker uses a pole. When a horse loses his balance, he raises his neck. A horse that *curls up*, though, usually has a training problem. Here are several reasons:

1 The rider is pulling on the reins and shortening the neck.
2 The horse is very sensitive and drops the bit (see Behind the Bit, p. 6).
3 The horse lacks power from the hind legs to support a double bridle and is balancing himself on the reins.

A curled-up horse may or may not be *behind the bit or behind the leg*.

DOWNHILL

When used to describe a horse, *downhill* refers to his balance. More weight is being carried on his front legs. Often, you see stiff or unbending hind legs and a "bouncing" croup. Too much tension in the back can also block the energy from the hind legs, resulting in a downhill balance.

DRIVING SEAT

The *driving seat* is an old style of riding. Modern horses are too sensitive, so don't try it. Your seat should just *follow* the horse's movement. You can sit *against* the movement to help your half-halt and you can *open* your seat to allow the horse to move more energetically forward with longer strides. But, do not sink your seat bones into the saddle and lean back; this drives the horse's back down. Study photos of the top modern riders.

ELASTICITY

Think of your horse's topline as a rubber band, able to shorten and lengthen with ease—this is *elasticity*. Visualize your horse's paces, from the shortest, highest trot (piaffe) to the trot that covers the most ground (extension). A correctly trained horse will be elastic and easily lengthened or shortened without resistance and without losing the correct rhythm.

ENGAGEMENT

This term is about a hind leg when it is the one on the ground. The *engaged* hind leg stays on the ground longer, with the horse lowering the croup and showing more bending in the joints of the hindquarters and the hind legs. This engaged hind leg carries the weight. Think of a coiled spring.

FLEXION

The word *flexion* means we are usually talking about the poll area. Look at the part of the horse from the crown piece of the bridle about 3 to 4 inches back; this is the poll area. A horse with too much *longitudinal* flexion will be *behind the vertical*. Correct *lateral* flexion prevents the horse's head from tilting and shows the horse is laterally supple all the way though his body. However, most horses usually don't want to flex to the left, so often when in a shoulder-in left, the poll is tilted (i.e. the horse is not stretching evenly into both reins). For example, a green horse on a 20-meter circle could be traveling to the left but flexing to the right. The poll is usually the last part of the horse to be laterally supple.

FORWARD

Old-style Warmbloods were very lazy, a bit dull, and not very sensitive in the back. Modern horses, however, with a more sensitive back and mind, have changed how training is addressed. Of necessity, in the old days, *forward* was the meat of every lesson, but not now. However, the obsession with forward has not quite left this country: too many people are running their horses off their feet and creating balance and tension issues. Forward means *direction*; it doesn't describe what we want from dressage. For example, a cross-country galloping horse is going forward but he is missing the elasticity and cadence that comes from true impulsion. I love an observation that FEI 5* Judge Stephen Clarke uses, "The more impulsion you have, the more submission you need." Keep this in mind!

FRAME

Refer to explanation in chapter 4 on page 53.

FROM BEHIND

Duh. Where else is the energy coming from? I don't use the term *from behind* too much when judging. Often, there is a submission issue, rather than an impulsion issue. Remember, submission comes before impulsion in the order of elements in the Training Pyramid. In fact, Number 2, *suppleness* and Number 3, *contact* are both related to submission. *Impulsion* is Number 4. When you are scoring 8s, then perhaps, you can think of more *from behind*! Judges often say "more from behind," but for lower-level riders, better comments could be used. A horse with hind legs pushing out behind, for example, would be better served with the comment "hind legs trailing" or "hind legs escaping."

HALF-HALT

It's such an overused word in dressage and in dressage lessons that you might well think the rider should be in a perpetual state of *half-halt*. A half-halt is a momentary influence of the aids that calls the horse to attention to warn him a new movement is coming up, or it's a momentary rebalancing that improves the collection. A half-halt is the perfect coordination of the driving aids, the bending aids, and the outside rein. In my book *Dressage for the Not-So-Perfect Horse* (Trafalgar Square Books, 2012) I discuss the variations of half-halts for each movement.

HEADSET

Headset describes a frame that is set with the horse holding himself there without suppleness or adjustability (also refer to On the Bit, p. 11).

HEAVY IN THE CONTACT

This usually has nothing to do with the horse's mouth, so a more severe bit won't help. It is an indication that his hind legs are not doing their job: they have either "escaped" the line of travel or they have fallen asleep. Sometimes, *contact is heavy* because the rider has not yet developed the skills to communicate correctly with the horse. She may need more education to improve her timing and seat so she can release the reins a bit. She also needs to learn to improve her half-halt. Often, a "heavy" horse has not been suppled laterally or is very crooked. When he is using the hind legs, all the energy can push down into the shoulders and into the contact.

IMPULSION

Impulsion is the willingness to go forward, quickly off the rider's leg with elasticity and ground-covering movement. Suppleness plays a huge part in impulsion: without a supple topline, impulsion is difficult to achieve.

INSIDE LEG

The rider's *inside leg* is placed at the girth to ask the horse to move forward, and it is placed one fist-length behind the girth to ask him to move sideways.

INSIDE LEG TO OUTSIDE REIN

Inside leg to outside rein is another phrase that is overused and misunderstood. The horse goes to the outside rein when he is asked to stretch and move or step toward it from the inside leg. It's not because the rider takes a good, strong hold on that rein and kicks with the inside leg. The horse can be put in a slight renvers position with his hind legs on the track and the forehand slightly to the inside, thus making the *outside* of the horse's body slightly shorter than the *inside*. This works well for a horse that likes to fall on the outside shoulder. The horse can also be put in a shoulder-fore position with some inside bending, thus making the inside of the horse slightly shorter than the outside. Here, the horse will take his inside hind leg and move it to the outside and slightly more under the body. The shoulders will be positioned slightly in, thus putting the inside hind and the outside front leg more on the same line of travel, which improves his balance. (For more on this subject, see chapter 9, p. 101.)

INSIDE REIN

It's not the "bad" rein. By "bad" I am referring to the fact that some instructors tell their students that it's all about the *outside* rein, and not to "touch" the *inside* rein. But, dressage is about correct use of *both* reins to create correct contact. The inside rein must be used in harmony with all the aids. It is used as a turning aid, and to bend or displace the neck and shoulders to the inside of the line of travel. The inside rein should not cross the neck (*inside rein of opposition*) as this position is not used in dressage. The inside rein should always be slightly away from the neck.

LATERAL

Lateral indicates side-to-side flexibility (suppleness, and the ability to create more or less bending).

LIGHTNESS

Lightness refers to the elevation and mobility of the shoulders, *not* how much weight the rider has in the reins.

LINE OF TRAVEL

It's necessary to straighten and collect the horse. Only two movements have the fore-hand on the *line of travel*: travers and half-pass. All other movements have the hind legs on the line of travel with the shoulders slightly displaced. The line of travel and the bend help the rider to create engagement of the hind legs. Piaffe, passage, one- and two-tempi changes, and rein back have the horse totally straight as both hind legs are carrying weight equally.

LONGITUDINAL

Longitudinal refers to topline flexibility (suppleness and the ability to lengthen and shorten the frame).

ON THE AIDS

When the horse is *on the aids*, horse and rider are communicating in harmony.

ON THE BIT

This is not a headset (see p. 9). A headset is non-adjustable because the head and neck stay in the same place, period. When I rode Western Pleasure, I was taught how to put my horse in a headset. The judges would mark you down if you had a horse that changed the frame during the class. Dressage is all about adjustability, which is why we don't have the headset. When the horse is truly *on the bit*, the rider has the ability to raise and/or lower or lengthen the neck (think of the "stretchy-chewy circle"—see p. 13), make the horse straighter in the neck, or be able to bend the neck more. The term *on the bit* doesn't just refer to the head and neck as *headset* does. *On the bit* really addresses the *entire* topline of the horse, which is why *suppleness* and *contact* in the Training Pyramid are so closely linked.

ON THE FOREHAND

When the horse is *on the forehand*, it means the horse's front legs are carrying more weight than the hind legs.

OVERBENT

Overbent refers to *lateral* bending (side-to-side bending). The neck is detached from the shoulders and is bending inward too much; the shoulders fall to the outside.

OVERFLEXED

Overflexed refers to the horse being behind the vertical or curled-up (see pp. 6 and 8).

OUTSIDE REIN

The *outside rein* is in charge of the speed and the amount of bend in the horse's neck. It's the final part of the half-halt. Make sure you realize this rein is *not* more important than the *inside* rein or the other aids. All must work together in harmony.

PENDULUM OF ELASTICITY

When the *Pendulum of Elasticity* (see illustration below) is hanging straight down, it points to the horse's natural working gaits. As he begins gymnastic training (that is, when he can score 65 percent in a USEF Training Level Test) the rider can slowly start to "swing" the Pendulum. To the left the horse moves to shorter, higher strides; to the right, he moves to lengthenings in trot and canter—more ground-covering strides.

PUTTING HORSE IN FRONT OF THE LEG

The horse must have a quick reaction to the leg. Go! You want the horse active enough so you don't have to push him every stride, and balanced enough so you don't have to hold him in balance with your reins.

RHYTHM

Rhythm is about the repetition of the footfalls for each gait. Without rhythm, we don't have dressage in the classical sense *or* the competition sense.

SEAT BONES

Modern dressage does not use driving or heavy *seat bones*. The modern horse cannot take a heavy seat, which just drives his back down. We use our seat as an aid. The seat refers to the part of your body covered by your underwear. You can move your underwear to the right or left as a weight aid (note: no leaning with the upper body). The seat is like a three-point plug: two seat bones and your crotch. "Plug your seat into" your saddle as you would a three-point plug into a wall. If you "unplug" your crotch, you will fall backward behind the motion. If you unplug your seat bones, you will lean forward over the horse's shoulders.

SELF-CARRIAGE

Self-carriage describes a balance where the horse carries weight on the *hind* legs, with mobile shoulders and an elastic contact with the rider.

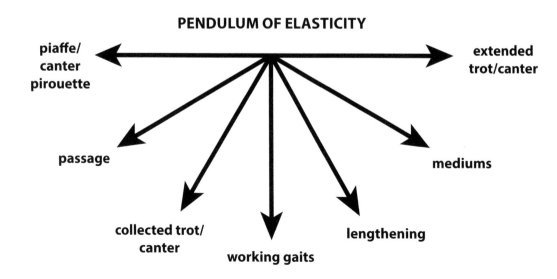

PENDULUM OF ELASTICITY

piaffe/canter pirouette ⟵⟶ extended trot/canter

passage

mediums

collected trot/canter

working gaits

lengthening

STRAIGHTNESS

Straightness is when the horse follows the line of travel. Let's go back to the German word for straightness: *Geraderichtung*. This one word translated correctly would take a whole sentence in English. The German word really means "straight riding" or "putting the horse on the line of travel"— that is, curved on curved lines and straight on straight lines.

STRETCH CIRCLE IN TROT

The *stretch circle in trot* is used for the warm-up and cool-down period of training and is also a good test to make sure your horse is adjustable and not rigid in the contact or in a headset. The horse softly chews the reins out of your hands, stretching forward and downward without losing balance or speeding up. The muscles of the horse's topline stretch and the suppleness in his back should improve. The contact should be such so that you still have an elastic feel with both reins. The horse should also be able to maintain the bend on the circle and not speed up.

SUPPLENESS

This is my favorite dressage word. Steffen Peters often says, "There is only one thing to think about. *Suppleness*, *suppleness*, and more *suppleness*." How true.

Think of your horse as like a freeway. There are two lanes of traffic. The lanes start with the energy of the hind legs; go up over the back, through the neck to the bit. Then the energy is sent back through the belly muscles to the hind legs. This is called the "circle of energy." So, if your freeway has a traffic accident or pothole (think of muscle tension in the back, or a stiff, short neck), why would you raise the speed limit? You must first clear the highway before the cars flow smoothly again. The rider needs to be a bit of a detective and find out where the stiffness and blockages are occurring. Can you bend more? Less? Can you put the neck higher? Lower? Can you go more forward? Can you do good transitions? The rider who never asks questions and just goes until there is a "traffic accident" will never be successful. On the other hand, the vigilant rider is always on the lookout for problems, always testing the suppleness, and will be successful.

TEMPO

Rhythm can be faster or slower; *tempo* refers to the rate of repetition of the rhythm. For example, the piaffe has the fastest tempo of the trots and the passage the slowest tempo. Both are still trots.

TILTED

Tilted means that the poll is not supple *laterally*, so the horse is not stretching evenly into both reins. A visual indicator is one ear higher than the other.

CHAPTER TWO

How Riders Learn

I have found over my 30 years of teaching that everyone learns differently. Children and young adults learn differently than adults: they do not seem to be afraid, while older, more mature riders do have a healthy dose of fear. Why a student is riding also plays a part in the way she learns. Does she want to compete? Does she just want to enjoy her horse? Or, is she doing it for status?

Being a good riding instructor takes practice, patience, and also a "knack" for teaching. Some amazing riders are terrible teachers and some average riders are excellent teachers. Styles of teaching and learning are different; the student and the teacher's styles need to mesh for the best learning opportunity. Some students like to be pushed, others like to be encouraged. A good teacher will learn several different methods and will be able to teach in the style that suits each student.

HOW TO LOOK FOR AN INSTRUCTOR

As the student looking for an instructor, the most important thing I can suggest is to go and watch a potential teacher give several lessons to riders at your same dressage level. See how the instructor handles the different situations. Would you feel comfortable with his or her teaching style?

Seek out a good learning environment. Is there a good sound system in the arena? It's important to hear your lesson! What about arena "traffic?" If you are a nervous rider or your horse is upset by a lot of horses in the ring at the same time, you may need to consider this. Make sure there is dust control for your own breathing as well as your horse's health. Footing is of the utmost importance.

Finances will need to be discussed. If showing is on the menu, then memberships and horse registrations must be budgeted. Talk about who will trailer the horse to competitions. How much will that cost?

How many days a week can you commit to riding the horse? How many lessons can you take each week? Will the trainer be schooling the horse, too? Be sure you are aware of all the financial obligations so there are never hard feelings.

GOAL-SETTING SESSION

I think a good teacher should always begin a new relationship by asking a new student about her past experience and where she and her horse are at the present. I like to find out the age, training, and athleticism of the horse and whether he has any limitations. What about the rider's seat and physical fitness? Is she willing to take longe lessons?

I also ask what her end goals are, and where she would like to see herself in a year. Having a reasonable timetable makes it more rewarding for both of us.

I, as the teacher, am the professional, so it is important in these goal-setting sessions to help guide a student to a logical and achievable plan. For example, if a student has been riding for just six months and has purchased a Grand Prix schoolmaster with the goal of showing at the Prix St. Georges level in one year, this is likely not a reasonable plan. But if I had agreed to that plan and the student failed, it wouldn't be the student's fault. And, since the horse is trained to Grand Prix, it wouldn't be the horse's fault either! I try to encourage a student's expectations to be realistic and to avoid failure of this sort.

It is also important to have a quarterly or a six-month review, just as you do with your financial advisor. Are goals being met or are you behind? If the latter, why? Sometimes a lameness of the horse, an illness of the rider, or other issues could have slowed progress. Is the horse having mental issue trying to meet the goals? Is your position holding you back? (If so, you need longe lessons.) Reviewing lesson plans can help progress.

On the other hand, there are some students who are happy to just enjoy

A HORSE'S LIMITATIONS

I always try to have honest discussions with my students who have horses that are either not the right size for them or horses that have limited physical ability. For example, when I have a 90-pound junior on a 17-hand, long horse, I must be honest and tell her that she will have difficulty collecting this animal, and that the "picture" isn't right. We must think of our horses as dance partners and we must "fit" together.

And, when a horse is willing but lacking in elasticity and natural balance, I need to discuss this with a student. Is it fair to the horse to try to keep working on collection and moving him up to Third Level, or should he be sold to someone else who would enjoy him and ride him at the level where he is confident and comfortable?

• STORY FROM THE ROAD •
Use Mistakes as Training Opportunities

Horses learn what they practice. If their riders allow them to ignore an aid, they think it is okay. Also be sure that when they are quick to respond, you praise them! Unless you reward and tell a horse he's a "good boy" when he is, he doesn't know it. Another thing dressage riders need to learn is that mistakes can happen. We all make them: riders, horses, trainers, and judges. An error gives us a chance to learn, or as my good friend Bill Solyntjes says, it's a "training opportunity."

My learning moment about mistakes came from Robert Dover, and bless him that he came into my life when he did. Someone who wanted me to stop the horse each time he made a mistake had trained me. Then, after the horse stopped, I was to turn around and do the movement again. Over and over if needed. The first lesson with Robert consisted of mostly him correcting my bad habits. He pointed out that in dressage we must always go forward and to do what I had been told by former trainers—that is, to stop when I created a reaction in my horse that was a mistake—is a really bad idea. The horse then learns to never go forward through a mistake, and we will pay the price as riders. Plus, stopping is a reward for the horse, so in a way you are actually rewarding the horse for the mistake.

Robert's plan was for me to figure out why the mistake happened. Was the neck too high? Too low? Was the horse crooked? On the shoulders? After I figured that out, I could fix the training issue then ride the movement again with ease. If you don't fix the problem that caused the mistake, you will just be making the same mistake over and over again.

their horses and have no desire to show or move up the levels. This type of student is fine with me, too. As long as anyone wants to learn and improve, I am okay with it. A few trainers I know won't teach this type of student because they feel frustrated by the lack of progress.

EACH LESSON NEEDS A PLAN

I always have a plan for each lesson. Of course, if an issue comes up during the lesson, the plan may need to be modified. If moving up one dressage level a year is the goal you have both agreed on, then your trainer needs to make lesson plans. How many new movements need to be taught to the horse and rider? How much more laterally supple does the horse need to be? How much more strength and carrying power needs to be developed for the horse to be in the correct balance for the next level? Remember, nothing can happen in 30 days! So I plan ahead and then work the plan.

I think it is important to give homework to my students. This helps to keep them responsible for the goals. I need to make sure they know *why* they must work on a certain issue, movement, or part of the Training Scale: I find students learn better— they might not be able to do it all the time, but knowing what they are aiming for is an important part of learning.

I am shocked at how many students come to me and don't know why they are riding a certain movement or exercise. They are used to the "traffic direction" lesson, where the trainer shouts out orders and an occasional, "Atta girl." Are these types of teachers just trying to keep their students dependent and tied to them? Perhaps.

I have told my students for 30 years that if they need someone to hold their hand, give them lessons every time they ride, and warm them up at every horse show, I am not their gal. I think having a lesson every day is a bad thing in the long run. The rider never has a chance to make a decision for herself.

Remember that making mistakes is part of learning. The horse will make mistakes, too. These are what I call "training opportunities." Without mistakes, no one learns. Don't be afraid of them; embrace them as great learning tools! Use your brain (the most important part of your body for dressage, by the way), and figure out to which aid the horse was not listening. Then work on an exercise that will reinforce that aid.

Some riders need honesty. This does not mean that the instructor can just tell them that they are bad riders. The instructor must be able to tell a rider that what she is doing is causing problems with the horse's training, then must be able to solve that problem and get the student going in the right way. Students are not dumb. To say, "Good, good," all the time isn't helpful. Be encouraging but honest.

A good teacher must be able to explain to the student whether or not what she is feeling and thinking is correct. Then the teacher must be able to teach the student correct feel.

MY TEACHING THEORY

My theory of teaching dressage is pretty simple. Work on the basics (see p. 6). When a rider has a good seat and the horse is trained well according to the Training Scale, the movements will take care of themselves. I encourage my students to audit clinics and also watch the lessons I teach to others when at home. Sometimes, I have them change horses to give them a different feel. I never tell them not to ride with someone else, though I suggest they go watch first if they can. Everyone has something to offer!

Dressage is very hard in that nothing we would do instinctively is correct for our sport. We use the reins first: when the horse falls out we try to pull him in with the inside rein, but this only makes him fall out more! The correct aid in this situation would be to counterflex the horse and use your outside leg to move his outside shoulder back to the inside. And, just repeating the wrong aid will never fix the problem; it just makes it worse. This is why a student must *think* first, then react until she has a better "feel" and more experience.

I know that I need to be able to sometimes explain an aid, a situation, and a movement more than 10 times or in many different ways. Let's say you are having a problem with the turn-on-the-haunches. I could have another student demonstrate. Visual learning like this is very good. Or, I could get on the horse and talk you through which aid I am using and what I feel the horse is doing in reaction to my aids. I can show you still photos (this works well when talking about balance or a correct frame), and videos are also good. I can create a few exercises that help you learn little bits and pieces of a movement. While working with all these teaching aids, hopefully, your light bulb will click on!

Back in the late 1970s, I was riding Triple Kema, a Third Level horse. I took a lesson from Linda Zang. She was teaching me about how the horse was falling on the outside shoulder, and she actually took a bat and gave him a couple of taps there. I did not get that at the time unfortunately. It wasn't until about four years later when trainer Uwe Steiner said, "You have to keep the shoulders up and mobile." Really? I am embarrassed to admit that I thought that if the hind legs were carrying, and the croup was lowered, the shoulders came up. I am sure all of my trainers were doing their job: they were teaching. I just wasn't doing my job: I wasn't learning!

MOVING UP THE LEVELS

I always look at a student's scores. When you have at least five rides at the highest test of a level over 63 percent, you are ready to move up. If you are only "Satisfactory" at 60 percent or below, you still have some holes in your training that need to be addressed.

Many times a student will tell me about her old trainer, and how things were done. I try never to criticize someone else, but say, "Okay, I understand but let's try a different approach and see how this works." Sometimes, with horses, you need to think outside the box, because not every horse learns the same way. This applies to humans, too!

WORKING WITH EMOTION

No matter what, when there is a lot of tension or fear, either in the rider or the horse, my lesson plan will need to be adapted. Tension or fear greatly interferes with the learning process. It is a very important job of the trainer to tell the rider that she must ride with *logic* and not emotion. Losing her temper with a horse might make her feel better for a short while, but it will do nothing for the training of the horse.

I found as a rider and trainer myself that it was much easier to ride *without emotion* on a client's horse. My own horse, not so much: I was convinced he sat up in his stall all night thinking of ways to avoid the flying changes! It took a few years for me to realize that emotion was not helping my training.

It takes a while to be mature enough to get to this point. Youngsters, especially in the teen years and early young adults, have more difficulty than most in handling their emotions. However, it is never permissible to lose your temper and punish the horse so I don't let students get away with it, and if they continue in this vein, I suggest that I'm not the right instructor for them.

I try to have a good enough relationship with my clients so that I can see at the beginning of a lesson where their emotional gauge is set that day. Are they upset? Afraid? Tired? In a good or bad mood? The answers to these questions can guide me as to how they will learn.

I always try to end the lessons on a good note with the horse and the rider, teaching them something new at the beginning and ending with something they both find enjoyable, whether that is a stretch circle, a short trail ride, or a few medium trots or canters.

TEACHING "FEEL"

Feel is very difficult to teach. It is about the rider responding correctly with her aids to problems she "feels" in the horse. I hear a lot of, "Do you feel that?" Often, the best thing I can do is ride her horse until it is soft and supple, then have the student

MY TEACHING RULES

To summarize, there are a few rules I live by when it comes to rider instruction and ensuring my students can learn:

1 Don't Yell

I use headsets or a mike. I love my radios and headsets! I have two receivers so my next student can put on her headset at the mounting block. This saves time between lessons. Teachers can get nodes on their vocal cords from overuse; these headsets help save my voice, and I love being able to hear the students communicate back to me. They are great on a windy or rainy day when outside noise interferes with the lesson; and when coaching at a show these are super, since no one wants to hear all the trainers yelling at their students!

2 Don't Be Too Nice

Some riders don't like to have their hands held and need honesty. This does not mean that I can just tell the student that she is a bad rider. An instructor must be able to tell the rider what she is doing that is causing problems with the horse's training. Then I must be able to solve that problem and get the student going in the right way. Students are not dumb. To say, "Good, good," all the time isn't helpful. I'm encouraging but honest.

3 Don't Be Afraid to Fire a Student

It doesn't happen often for me, but it has happened. I am happy to teach everyone who is willing to learn, no matter how slow they learn, and no matter at what level they are riding. I am happy to work with any breed or size of horse. What I will not tolerate is a student who blames and punishes the horse 100 percent for her own mistakes and has a nasty temper. I have even gone so far in an out-of-town clinic to tell the organizer to give that type of person her money back and ask her to leave. I did not charge for that lesson.

4 Give Positive Reinforcement

I'm always sure to give a lot of, "Atta girls!" I so much enjoy hearing Scott Hassler and Debbie McDonald say, "I LOVE THAT," in their lessons. I also never fail to have a box of sugar by my chair so I have the chance to give the horse a treat for his good work!

get on so she can "feel" the elastic contact and try to repeat that feeling over and over again. This practice is such a part of learning. However, practice only makes perfect *if* the practice IS perfect.

If the rider makes the wrong correction or reacts incorrectly, I then stop and talk about it and ask her what she felt. Then, I'll explain to her what the correct reaction to that feeling should be, and tell her what she needs to do to improve her aids and technique.

Slow It Down

When a rider is not getting the idea of "feel," I do not want her to continue in trot or canter. I ask her to walk, and work through the issue slowly. Remember how you learned to play tennis? The instructor did not just start throwing balls at you. First, he taught you the stance, then the pivot, the swing, and the step. When these movements, through practice, became more natural and effortless to the point your brain wasn't so overloaded, he started throwing balls at you.

I encourage a rider to think: better to walk a few minutes and think through an evasion than continue to do the wrong correction where the horse doesn't learn anything, the rider never gets better, and they just practice the same old bad habits.

GOOD SEAT AND POSITION

DRAWING A shows a rider with a correct position. The line from the shoulder/hip/heel is straight as is the line from the elbow/hand/bit. The shoulders are square and directly over the hips. There is a three-point contact position with the seat/saddle (two seat bones and crotch). There is a slight bend in the knee. The heels could be a bit lower, but they are level with the ball of the foot.

The rider in **DRAWING B** is not stable over the lower leg, as the lower leg has moved forward and the knee is too straight. This also causes the rider to perch more forward on the crotch, losing the three-point contact with the seat/saddle.

The rider in **DRAWING C** has her stirrups too long. There must be a bend in the knee of the rider, or the rider will lose one of the shock absorbers. This rider has the look of "standing in the stirrups" rather than "sitting on the horse."

In **DRAWING D**, the rider is not only standing in the stirrups but has also hunched over her shoulders. With this position the rider will not have an elastic contact nor will she be able to correctly use her core. This horse will usually have a short neck and a stiff contact.

DRAWING E shows a rider who has moved her lower leg back too far, which then tilts her upper body forward. She will be balancing on a gripping thigh, and will not be able to have an elastic contact. This type of position will cause the energy of the horse to move backward, and the horse will usually have a short neck and a stiff contact.

In **DRAWING F** the rider is leaning back and will have no ability to ride a correct half-halt, and will usually balance only on the reins. She will be behind the movement of the horse and will be unable to ride correct half-halts.

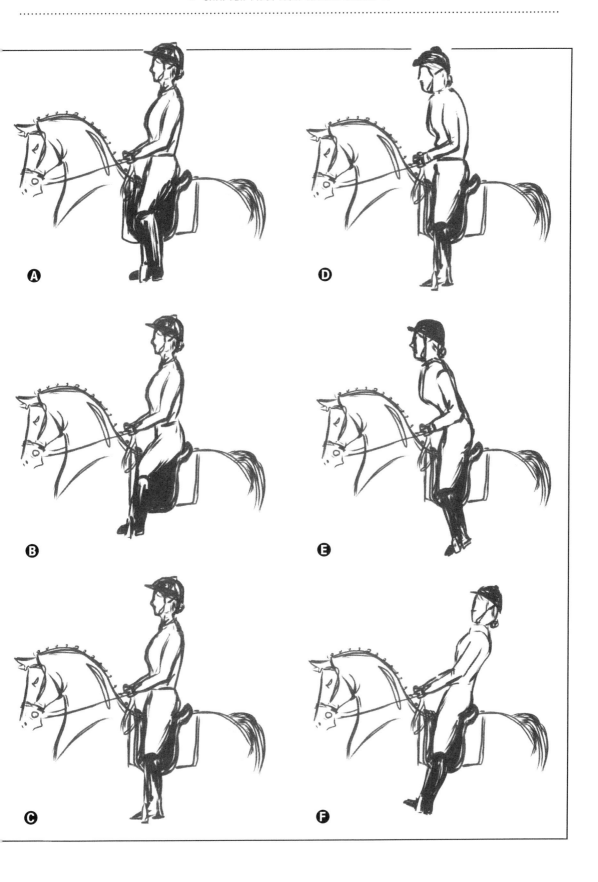

PROMOTING A GOOD SEAT AND POSITION

When I'm giving a clinic, I am always amazed to hear a new student say, "My regular instructor does not give longe lessons." REALLY? I quickly suggest she finds another teacher.

I realize that sometimes the rider's horse is not suitable for a lesson of this sort. When I had my main training barns, I always had a wonderful longe horse there, but not every instructor is so fortunate. Perhaps you can ask other instructors in your area if they have a longe horse, and go to their barn for longeing instruction.

A good instructor should not be so selfish or paranoid about suggesting assistance from another professional when unable to help.

The Benefit of a "Professor" Horse

When a student can lease or buy a "teacher" horse—that is, a schoolmaster—to me, this is the best of all worlds. The rider can get a feel for the movements and have a great learning opportunity. Remember, however, that you cannot jump from Training Level to Fourth Level just because the horse knows his stuff. You must spend time on your technique and learn how to ride transitions, understand the new movements, and find out how to properly collect the horse.

As a judge, I see too many fantastic schoolmasters ridden above the level of competency of the rider. With this pair, I will give the horse a "5" on Submission and the rider a "4." I often wonder who teaches these types of riders. Perhaps the rider is doing it on her own, or perhaps a trainer has tried to tell her not to do it, and she didn't listen. I always feel badly as a judge when I have to impart this knowledge to the rider.

~ PROBLEMS ~
and Solutions

Q **I've struggled with the concept that you need to be uncomfortable sometimes in order to progress. Do you agree?**

A Right on! You do need to be a bit out of your comfort zone to progress, and so does the horse. The key to a good trainer and rider, however, is to know just how far to push the horse without destroying his confidence and willingness to work. I often tell my students that there are two athletes in this sport, and they both need to sweat a bit more.

Q **I sometimes feel stupid during a lesson when I don't understand what my instructor is telling me. For example, she told me my horse was "dropping a shoulder." I didn't have any idea what she was talking about. I felt embarrassed to tell her that I didn't understand, especially when there were other people observing my lesson. Is it okay to interrupt a lesson to ask my questions, or should I wait until after the lesson is over, find the answer in a book, or ask a friend?**

A Remember, *you* are paying the instructor. This means he or she is your employee, and you are the boss. I am a bit worried about your relationship with your instructor if you feel you can't have open and honest communication. You should not wait to ask because you'll miss that learning opportunity—when it has just happened, it is the best time to stop and say, "I am sorry, could you explain that to me? I don't understand." You should not be embarrassed. In

fact, those watching will no doubt be grateful as well, as they might not understand what he or she is saying, either! You will never improve if you don't get immediate information to help develop your feel and your skills. The teacher will just assume you understand everything unless you speak up!

Q **I am a relative newbie at dressage. The concepts of Impulsion, Contact, and riding with your seat were terms that took me a long time to intellectually understand. Now, if I could just physically do them… !**

A Steffen Peters often says the most important part of the rider's body for dressage is the brain. I agree. When you can *think*, you will get better. Dressage is logical training for the horse and rider. Keep it simple. Your brain must train your body to make the correct aid—reactions must become automatic.

Q **My current sticking point is, what does it take to move from being a mid-level rider to an upper-level rider? Please be more specific than just saying, "More of everything."**

A Knowledge and more knowledge! Better timing. A correct seat. An upper-level rider cannot get away with being crooked. She also needs a much better level of fitness than at Training Level. Some trainers say it gets easier as you move up the levels, but I don't agree. It gets different, but remember, you only have three aids for all of those movements, so body control, knowledge about the movements, and how to apply the aids are of utmost importance.

Q **I see riders flopping around in the saddle like sacks of potatoes. Their hands and legs are flying everywhere and the thing that bugs me most is the amount of "bobble heads." I only wish that they would learn to really stay still! What can you suggest?**

A I think riders need to realize that their own suppleness entails having enough strength in their muscles so that they are able to sit quietly and still. It doesn't take much strength to be a "bobble head," but it takes a lot of muscle and core strength to sit still and look elegant. I think some of this is the result of many riders not wanting to get fit!

Q **As an older adult, I have some hearing loss. Frequently, during a lesson, my instructor will tell me to do something, but I can't understand her. Sometimes, I ride over to ask, but it happens so frequently I just give up and keep riding. When I first started lessons, I did mention my hearing loss, and I feel uncomfortable telling her every time. What do you suggest?**

A I have some hearing loss too, and I bought two sets of the headsets to use mainly because I could not hear my students trying to communicate with me when there was rain or wind. I love these because now I can talk softly to a student (rather than using just a megaphone or mike) and I can hear her all the time. It's a win-win!

Talk to your instructor's other students and see if they have the same problem, then perhaps you could all pitch in for a headset system for a birthday or holiday gift. If that doesn't work, then I suggest you buy your own headsets, as you are wasting your lesson money now if you really can't hear your instructor.

Q **Is it better to concentrate on learning one aid at a time, or in combination? If one at a time, which one should I start with? My horse is very eager to please so I don't need to discipline as much as teach her.**

A Learning the aids is a bit like taking singing lessons: you first need to read the notes and be able to carry a tune before you can sing in harmony. So, you need to be clear what each aid does, and how the horse should react to it. You should know the Training Scale so you also understand where in order of importance each aid is positioned. Then, as you gain experience, you will be able to work more and more in harmony with your horse. Be patient. Things take time.

Q **How do you help a student get over extreme anxiety?**

A If you suffer from nerves, the best thing is a lot of practice and preparation. When you know you have ridden a test successfully at home ten times, you are ready to go to the show. I suggest you take your horse to the showgrounds the first few times and just pay a schooling fee so you can work in a relaxed manner.

Don't put the pressure of a test coming up at 3:00 p.m. on your shoulders. Make sure you and your horse are confident in the show setting, then start with a schooling show. If your horse doesn't like indoor arenas, don't take him to a show held in one. Does your horse like to see other horses? Find grounds where this is possible. Note: A sure recipe for disaster is to take his best friend along, too, and leave him in the stall "screaming" for your horse while you are in the ring.

Q How do I find a good instructor and know I am getting what I am paying for?

A I think you need to go and watch some lessons and audit clinics. First, you need to find a teacher whose style you like. I never mind when someone asks if she can come and watch my lessons to "check me out." If an instructor objects to this, cross her off your list.

It is also good to find out what the instructor has accomplished. Has she attended an "L" Program or USDF Instructor Workshop? What sort of record does she have in the show arena? What have her students accomplished? Who does she take lessons from herself?

Being a good detective is important to make sure you are not getting into a bad deal. I have seen some people falsely advertising themselves, but with the Internet this is not as easy to pass off it used to be. Google is your new best friend!

Your new teacher should be willing to sit down with you and discuss your goals.

Q Isn't the dressage community failing miserably at developing thinking riders? And, why are we riders doing what we are doing? Showing should not be the reason.

A I agree that riders need to remember that the brain is the most important part of the body when riding dressage! Also emotions should be checked at the door. Horse training should be *logical*. Many riders don't think for themselves, they just wait for the trainer to tell them what to do. I believe trainers are making their students too dependent on them—even coaching them every time right before they go into the show ring.

I know of some trainers who do not take students that don't want to show. For me, as a trainer and instructor, I just require a student who wants to learn and has empathy for her horse. It doesn't matter to me if they show or not. And it doesn't matter to me if they want to move up the levels or not. We set goals, and then I try to help my students achieve that goal.

Q When my trainer asks, "Did you 'feel' that?" and I didn't (I'm still new to dressage), how can she help me develop that skill?

A You need to be honest with your trainer and tell her you don't understand. As teachers, we need your feedback so we can say it in another way or perhaps go down a different track. The only way we really have to teach "feel" is for us to say, "That is the right look," or "That is how the horse should feel," then have you try to replicate the feeling.

Remember that you are learning new techniques and often this will feel different to you, but "different" is not always wrong. This is why having a good trainer is important to help guide you along with these changes.

Q **How long of a leg is ideal? I have seen legs so straight it looks like the rider is standing.**

A I do think many riders have their stirrups too long. There needs to be a clear bend in the knee so the rider can keep the lower leg back underneath the hip. You should think of the perfect position as standing on the horse in a bent knee position.

Q **Don't you think that riders should have a Training Pyramid, just like the horse? It makes no sense to me that only the horse has to follow a Training Scale and the rider gets a "free" ride, so to speak.**

A Here you go, the Rider Training Pyramid from my book *Dressage for the Not-So-Perfect Horse*:

Q **I have had many lessons and I continue to do the same things over and over. I keep practicing and keep doing it wrong. Is there something you do to really change an ingrained habit?**

A There have been studies done with other sports about how many repetitions it takes to end a habit or to make a new one. It is in the thousands. So breaking a bad habit and creating a new one will take some time. You don't tell me which habit you would like to break, but let's use holding your hands too high as an example. Try to pick four places in your arena where you only think about your hands, and move them back to the correct position. You must do this every time you go by A, C, B, and E. You need perfect practice to be able to use that old phrase, "Practice makes perfect!"

Harmony, invisible aids, and a wonderful partnership

Effective rider with good influence and tact

Effective rider with fairly good influence

Rider has correct position but lacks correct influence (rider a bit of a passenger but does not inhibit performance)

Rider lacks correct position

Q Do your arms belong to you or your horse?

A I would say your position belongs to *you* and your horse needs to learn to come to your position rather than you having to follow him around. If the horse is always pulling your arms out, you need to make sure you are riding him correctly, keeping him straight, and using your transitions and exercises to keep him in balance. He has four legs and you have only two arms; he needs to know you are not a fifth leg for him! Make sure you are balanced over your lower legs, and that you are using your upper leg and core correctly to help your leverage.

Q Where can I go to improve my teaching? What are the hallmarks of a good teacher?

A The USDF Instructor Workshops do have a session on teaching. I was lucky to go through the British Horse Society system, which places a lot of emphasis on teaching and lesson planning. We had to teach many group lessons, which hardly anyone does anymore. A good teacher needs to have empathy for his or her students and know that most people do not learn well when yelled at and put under too much pressure. On the other hand, the teacher must gently push the student along at times. Sometimes with a difficult lesson or student, I think to myself, "I am doing my job, I am teaching, but the student is not doing her job, she is not learning." This happens rarely, and as long as my students are trying, I am 100 percent supportive of their efforts.

Q I think if you are discussing the imperfect rider, looking at human body conformation can be helpful. I remember being confused by advice given on the discussion boards, then realized it was because of varying shapes and sizes of riders. Telling me to sit up only makes my seat worse! What are your thoughts about rider conformation?

A I always struggled with short arms. When I was told to have my elbows on my hips, it was difficult for me to get my hands out in front of me rather than in my lap. It did not feel natural. Finally, I had a teacher with short arms, and she told me to move my elbows in front of my hips and not have as much bend in my elbows.

I wish I was tall and blond and elegant like Christine Traurig, but I am not. I am thrilled that my body is much like Debbie McDonald's and she always looks so elegant on a horse. We all need to know our own body and our own limitations but still keep striving for the most elegant look we can get.

Q My trainer wants me to have a lesson every day and also wants to school me before every class at the show. Is this okay?

A Well, I do think many trainers make their students too dependent on them. Students need to be able to think on their own. A lot of the learning process is about making mistakes, and this includes our horses. I also think trainers don't explain things in enough detail, rather, they just give orders. I don't think anyone improves with this style of teaching. You need to know *how* the horse works, *why* the trainer is asking you to do something, and *how* that will correctly influence the horse.

So if you are a very green rider and you are learning on a schoolmaster, perhaps constant supervision for a while is a good thing. But remember, you do need some time to practice and work on your skills on your own. As far as coaching at the show, this can be helpful for many people. My students never benefitted much from it, however, because I was always on a horse myself, getting ready for a class. I am afraid I just threw them to the wolves at the show! But, I did have a great group of students who did very well in competition, and were quite independent.

Q **Can you discuss how a rider uses her legs differently in half-pass, travers, and shoulder-in?**

A For the long answer, I suggest you go to *Dressage for the Not-So-Perfect Horse* and read chapters 9, 10, and 15. There is a huge amount of information there. This book will also tell you which leg needs to be active at what time—depending on the horse's evasions.

But, for a short answer, remember that in shoulder-in the horse is bent *moving away* from the direction of the bend, and in half-pass and travers, he is bent *into the direction* of travel. The aids in brief:

Shoulder-in: Inside leg is at the girth to ride the horse forward and to help keep the bend. Outside leg is behind the girth to keep the haunches from falling out. The inside leg is the active leg and you should sit either in the middle of the horse or to the inside of the bend.

Half-pass and travers: Inside leg is at the girth to keep the bend and activity of the inside hind. Outside leg is behind the girth; this leg is active in the half-halt to tell the horse to displace his haunches to the inside, and to move sideways in the half-pass. Your weight is in the direction of the bend.

Q **I am having trouble at the canter. How can I improve the canter exercises?**

A When an exercise is failing at the trot or canter, go to walk. Remember the tennis lesson (see p. 22): one small step at a time. Allow yourself time to think and time to make a good correction at the walk. And if you are fearful, remember walk is the best place to approach a correction!

Q **I think one of the most difficult concepts to grasp is that each rider needs time to understand what she is hearing, feeling, and seeing. There is no quick path to understanding. There are only steps, usually taken one at a time, and not always in any particular order, that will eventually take you to a new level of knowledge. As with life in general, we probably won't fully understand until we approach the end of the process, will we?**

A Yes, dressage is a lifelong journey, for sure! I wish I had the body of a 25-year-old and the knowledge I have accumulated over the years. But it doesn't work that way. So I just do the best I can to share what I have learned and try to make others' path a bit easier.

....

Q **What are your suggestions for improving my half-halt? Do I start with the reins? Help me learn to "feel" this!**

A *Coordination* and *feel* are hard to learn (and also hard to teach)! I like to start every half-halt with the closing of my upper leg. First, this warns the horse something is coming, second, it gives me more leverage and secures my seat and position just in case the horse decides to pull or run instead of responding to the half-halt.

I then make sure there is enough energy coming from the hind legs. It is difficult at first not to grab the horse with your lower leg too, as you firm up the thigh. Remember, the lower leg still has to be a bit "breathing," not gripping. I then check the suppleness in the contact, with a little bit of flexing to the inside or outside, strengthen my core, and also use the outside rein if needed to sit momentarily "against" the horse in order to bring the hind legs a bit closer to the mouth.

This stronger feeling should only last for a moment or a stride or two. Do not try to stay there until the horse gives in. You will not be strong enough and it is not the right idea anyway. If the horse responds you release and relax for a moment and allow more self-carriage. If there is no response or an incorrect response, then it is time to be a detective and figure out which aid the horse is not responding to, and go back and work on a correct reaction to that aid. Was it the leg? Was the horse crooked? Lazy? Stiff to the bend? Locked in a bend? Lacking suppleness

in the contact? Any of these will prevent a correct half-halt from working.

....

Q **How do I become a feeling rider, with the balance of giving and taking? When I use my reins, should I ever take them backward? When should I give?**

A In dressage, there is very little taking back on the reins. You want to think of creating a "barrier" with the reins, though some energy must always be allowed to come through the reins, as dressage is always forward-thinking. Think of your reins as perhaps being a bit like Swiss cheese at first, then more like cheesecloth as the horse's training progresses, so more energy will be contained as training and collection progresses.

The most important thing is not the "front door," but rather the activity of the horse's hind legs and the ability of the rider to create a supple topline in the horse, which can conduct the energy to the reins. A rider should have about 2 to 5 pounds in each rein, with an elastic and supple contact. The weight changes a bit all the time depending on the gait and also the suppleness of the horse. When the horse is equal in both reins and accepting a supple and elastic contact, then a reward of "giving" is appropriate.

The key to the half-halt is *not* waiting to do one until the horse tests you—a good rider should always be testing her aids *before* the horse gets ahead of her!

Q **What specific skills does the rider need to develop as she progresses up the levels? What things will help the learning process? Too often, riding skills are presented as an all-at-once thing, when realistically that's not possible.**

A You are totally correct: things take time. First, you need to work on the longe line and develop the best possible seat you can. This is really the "meat" of the process. Once your position is stable, you can begin to develop your aids correctly. As you move up the levels, it becomes more and more important that you are able to maintain a correct position and sit in the middle of the saddle. I often see riders who sit well as long as the horse is submissive, but once there is some resistance, they start kicking and pulling, which usually makes things worse!

Work on correct timing of the aids and correct half-halts is a lifetime process. Even in High Performance Clinics, the coach is always reminding the riders about little details. "Sit deeper," "Give more," or "Less curb rein." So, the journey is long, rewarding, and, in a way, never-ending!

Q **How do the dressage movements fit into my riding?**

A Think of the movements as pieces of a jigsaw puzzle. They are all important and without them you will not see the big picture. If you were doing a puzzle, you would do the edge pieces first. Then you would say, "Oh, the sky is blue and the grass is green." You then sort all those pieces and know where they should fit. The

movements are like that, too. If you think of riding Grand Prix as the fairy princess in the castle tower of your puzzle, you will see how you can't get there until all the other little pieces are fitting in the right spot.

Q **Tell me about the canter depart!**

A For horses and people, doing the right-lead depart, then the following circle, is often difficult. Why?

First, most horses and most people are right-handed. This means they are more coordinated on their right side and stronger on their left sides. So horses and riders like to drift left when going right. Now, we all know the right lead canter starts on the left hind. So, in order to get the right lead canter, the rider must make sure she has control of the left hind leg. A little counterflexing, with a bit of a leg-yield to the right should be done prior to the depart to make sure the outside barrier is up. As the rider does this, she should also make sure she steps with her own weight more into the inside stirrup.

Once the horse is cantering, the rider should be careful not to allow the horse to bend too much to the inside or *right*, as this will allow the horse to push the muscles back out to the left into the outside leg. It will be difficult for you to sit to the right when this happens. Better to keep the green or young horse slightly counterflexed this direction, so you have a place to sit on the right.

Once you come off the circle, there is another danger spot, so before you leave the circle, it is a good idea to again test that outside barrier; once you leave the circle, the tendency is for the horse to push left into his strong side to help his balance on the straight line. Unfortunately, in canter this often results in the loss of the lead behind, or the horse breaks to trot.

Q **I am new and need a good instructor. What do I look for?**

A I think that an instructor at the very beginning levels must tell you about the "big picture," but also explain how you, as well as the horse, must learn the small pieces first. The idea of riding good dressage is about training correct *reactions* in the rider as well as the horse.

Q **I think the seat for First Level does not have to be as educated as for Second Level. And you need to be more educated to influence the bend and the gaits in Third and Fourth Levels. In what ways does your seat need to be more educated as you move up the levels? What happens if my seat is faulty?**

A Your "aids"— not just your seat—need to be more sophisticated as you move up the levels. But, if your horse is a school-master, and you sit only to the left, you will have difficulty at First Level keeping him on the right lead on a straight line. Your weight aids will confuse him, and he will, no doubt, throw in a lot of flying changes! So, I highly recommend longe lessons at the beginning, even if you are only showing and schooling Training Level.

I covered the use of the aids (legs, seat, hands) for every movement, in depth, in my first book *Dressage for the Not-So-Perfect Horse.*

Q **I get so confused about where my horse is evading my aids. Help me find a better way to figure this out!**

A Try to keep it simple: One aid, one answer. Take a look at the definitions of aids, bending aids, inside leg to outside rein, and outside rein on pages 5, 6, 10, and 11. Read about the aids and what they should do and what the horse's reaction should be. Remember, we only have three aids: our seat, hands, and legs.

Q **I cannot understand the concept of "opening up the hips" or visualize how to do it.**

A "Opening the hips" is not something that feels natural, unless you are a dancer or gymnast and have done a lot of stretching with the idea of stretching the top of your thigh and front of your hip. Think about doing a back bend. In everyday life, no one does back bends for anything; if you drop something on the floor, you lean for-ward and pick it up.

When in the saddle, just walking on your horse, take your ankle in your hand and pull your thigh so it is perpendicular to the ground. Point your knee straight down to the ground. Now take your shoulder back and think about pulling on your ankle as you do it. In other words, you will be doing a bit of a back bend while on the horse. This type of stretching will help to loosen you up and give you a better feeling for "opening the hips" when you start your work session.

Q How do I improve my timing?

A Through practice and making mistakes! As I've already mentioned, too many trainers make their students too dependent on them and never allow the students to think on their own. A lot of learning is about making mistakes, and that is how we all learn, including the horse!

Q How does incorrect riding ruin dressage?

A Good question. Not many riders think about this; they are more concerned about their horse and whether the horse is doing *his* job. I find there are a great many riders at Second Level and above who are still very crooked in the saddle. The other day in a Prix St. Georges class a rider was leaning so far left in her approach to a *right* canter pirouette, the horse had no chance—needless to say, the horse changed the lead to the left lead before the pirouette. This was unnoticed by the rider, so she did a small circle on the wrong lead, then proceeded to "C" where she actually gave an aid for a flying change. I had to give her a "4" or "Insufficient" for the rider mark, because it was *the rider*, not the horse being resistant, that created the mistakes. This is the worst type of example of what can happen when a rider is not up to the standard.

A crooked rider can have a negative influence on the half-pass, the flying change, and the counter-canter because it's impossible for the horse to stay engaged on the correct hind leg if the rider cannot sit over it. Also, a rider with very unstable and banging lower legs creates regularity issues in the medium and extended trots. Riders with an unstable seat use the reins too much, and their horses lose impulsion, suppleness, and can have mouth problems.

CHAPTER THREE

How Horses Learn

I f you have never trained a horse from scratch, you need to understand how a horse learns. In many clinics I have riders tell me their horse won't—or can't—do some movement or other, but usually the horse would be happy to do it, if he only understood what the heck the rider really wanted.

I like to tell people that training horses is like teaching children to read. You first teach them the ABCs. Then, you teach them words. Next, the children can work on concepts trying to string these words together and finally, after quite a long education, they are ready to read a book. Remember the "Dick and Jane" books? Perfect for that stage. Obviously, no parent or teacher would ask their child who does not know his ABCs to read a college-level textbook. However, there are many riders who think their horse should be able to "read a textbook" after only a few months of training him.

START AT THE BEGINNING

Ahead, I will basically go through all the aids the horse needs to know in order to read his first book. When you read this chapter, ask yourself, "Are there pieces here I have neglected to explain to my horse?" If so, now is the time to do it! Remember, each dressage movement is like a jigsaw puzzle, made up of many responses to the different aids. How will the horse understand the big picture if you have not explained the puzzle pieces and put them properly into place? When there are holes in a horse's education, there will be resistance and confusion.

First Words: Longeing

Before I ever sit on a horse, I teach him to be longed. I always use side-reins with a horse that wants to be too low in the neck, or Vienna reins, which are best for teaching a young horse to stretch over his back and to lower a high neck. I never just allow him to run around like a maniac on the longe line. First, it is dangerous; second, when a horse is wearing tack, I want him to recognize it means work.

MOM AND PLAYMATES

Foals learn from their moms and from other playmates. I had one broodmare who was the sweetest thing in the world. She let her foals jump all over her, and they were obviously in charge. It was interesting that when we backed these foals, they were always a bit more difficult. Used to being in charge, they did not want to allow a mere human to be in control!

Another mare I owned was just a witch: I left a halter on her at all times, and we were never able to get near her babies for at least 24 hours after foaling. One afternoon, I drove up to the barn, and the vet had gone into her stall without me. I saw him leaping over the top of the Dutch door with Miss Electra right after him—ears pinned! Her foals however, were so easy to back as they all were used to toeing the line.

Playmates in the pasture also teach foals a pecking order and how to socialize with others. I am not sure that horses learn bad or good habits from their friends. It would be nice if they could learn that way: we could just stand them by the dressage arena and have them watch a Grand Prix horse. Maybe they would think that was a good idea, too!

At this point, it is ideal if you have a round ring because it is very difficult to teach a horse to balance when he wants to fall in or fall out on the circle all the time. The best thing for a young horse is to have a solid wall to "lean on" around the 20- to 25-meter circle.

With longeing, you are teaching the horse basic voice commands: "Walk," "Trot," "Canter," and "Whoa." Perhaps, in addition, you can make a little noise or use your voice saying, "Easy…" to help slow and calm him down. When I step in front of my horse's eye, and put out my arm (not the arm holding the line) and say, "Whoa," he should halt.

Keep your standards high here and don't let him turn in and face you. Keep pointing the longe whip at the girth when you "Whoa" to help him understand this concept. (The whip at the girth will later become your inside leg in the saddle.)

The horse should move off quickly when you ask; if he doesn't, use the longe whip near his hindquarters. I am against a lot of snapping of the longe whip (like a lion-tamer) because I think this will "deaden" him to your driving aids. Remember, you will be using your voice aids to associate your leg, seat, and rein aids when you are mounted.

This is the first part of the ABCs: *Go* and *stop*; you will teach the horse to *turn* when you are mounted.

Longeing with a Rider

Once the horse is longeing in balance and can quietly make all the transitions and feel comfortable using his topline, then it is time to add the weight of a rider (while still on the longe line). Make sure the person in charge of the line and whip is experienced because you will need her help to keep you (the rider) safe, and give your horse a good learning experience.

When I'm doing the longeing, I usually don't give the rider the reins at first, but just sit her on the horse and use my voice aids to get the horse's reaction, and to get him used to balancing well with the additional weight. Once he is comfortable with this, you can remove the side-reins or Vienna reins and give the reins to the rider. Of course, this rider must be someone with an excellent seat and position.

Off the Longe

Now, with the horse off the longe, spend a few days in the round ring with you (or the person who was longeing) standing in the middle while the rider uses her voice to associate her leg, seat, and rein aids with the *go* and *stop*. Then it's time to venture out into the large arena. I often like to have an experienced horse there, and we play a little game of "baby elephant train": the experienced horse goes first, and you "park" the young horse behind him. This helps to keep him going forward but also at a steady pace. I usually don't canter in the big arena for a while until we work a bit on steering and turning.

Since the horse is already accepting the contact easily from longeing, where he learns it through proper use of side-reins, it is no effort to put him on the bit. That work is done! He needs to get comfortable with the different leg and seat aids for the three gaits.

Aids for the Gaits

Walk: Use alternating seat and leg aids. Use your *lower* leg as the horse's rib cage swings into it. Remember that since the walk has no impulsion you cannot drive the horse more forward with your seat; instead you use your leg quickly or use a tap with the whip behind the leg at the correct moment.

Trot: Your seat moves equally forward toward your hands and your inside leg stays at the girth as the *go* aid.

Canter: Your weight moves to the inside seat bone and works a bit like you are on a swing, in a slight scooping motion. The inside leg at the girth keeps the horse cantering—that is, it's still a *go* aid. The outside leg behind the girth is the leg that tells the horse to canter along with the movement of your weight and seat aid. Remember, the canter stride starts with the outside hind leg, and for a young horse this outside leg will be very important. (Later, when he has learned travers or head-to-the-wall leg-yield, then he may be confused by too much outside leg, which is when you will need to make your inside leg and your seat more important.)

At this point, the horse is equally stretching into both reins and is fairly straight, but doesn't know how to bend. So the next step is the *turn*.

Turning Aid

You use your inside rein to lead the horse's neck and shoulders to the inside. Use it like a turn signal: give and take. Move your weight in the direction of the turn. Use your outside leg forward at the girth as a little tapping aid, so the horse moves away from the leg under your weight. This aid will become more sophisticated later.

Now you are ready for some large circles and changes through the diagonal. Your horse will, no doubt, fall in going in one direction and fall out on the other. However, you can't fix this until you teach him another aid—the lateral-moving leg aid (see below). Do not try to pull the horse in or out with your reins.

Moving Sideways Off the Leg

Remember that until now the horse only understood that pressure from your inside leg means to go forward. Many riders at this stage don't teach the horse the *lateral-moving* leg aid; rather, they impatiently start pulling him out with the inside rein. Teaching the horse to move laterally off either of your legs also improves your canter departs and helps to ensure the horse takes the correct lead. He must learn to *move sideways off your inside leg (outward)* and *sideways off your outside leg (inward)*.

During the horse's training I do a lot of work from the ground, which is how I like to start teaching this moving-sideways aid. I stand near the girth, and bend the horse slightly toward me with the inside rein. Then I take the butt of the whip and tap him right behind the girth where my leg will be when mounted. If there is no reaction, I tap harder until the horse steps away from the whip. Then I reward him.

Remember, he should move quickly away from a light pressure from the whip, as this is the reaction you want from your leg.

Once the horse has worked in both directions, you now have an aid that he understands; you can teach him the turn-on-the-forehand, which is the most basic lateral exercise for the horse because there is no forward motion involved. If he still seems confused with this aid, ask your ground person to help you.

YOUR HORSE CAN READ!

With the *go*, *stop*, *turn*, and *move sideways* aids your horse now has a basic understanding of the simple aids of dressage. From these basic aids he can learn the more complicated exercises. However, when he acts confused, don't punish him or just give a stronger aid. Think about his understanding. Is it clear to him what you are asking? Should you go back and review the aids to make sure? This is always a good idea, in my opinion. All of the movements usually come back to those simple ABCs!

SCIENTIFIC LEARNING

Scientists talk about "conditioning." The horse can certainly be "conditioned" over time to respond in a desired (or in some cases, undesired) way. You use an aid until he responds. When he responds correctly, you use *negative reinforcement* (removal of the stimulus—that is, you cease the aid) and perhaps *positive reinforcement* (the addition of a rewarding stimulus, such as a pat or verbal praise). On occasion there might be cause for momentary *punishment* or *correction* (a tap with the whip, a stronger rein aid) to get the horse's attention. Remember that for the horse to learn correctly, the rider must be quick to give positive and negative reinforcement, and regain the horse's attention with a correction when necessary. Do not just keep asking, asking, and asking as this will make him dull. Remember that you are smarter and the horse is stronger. You will never "make" a horse do anything!

ARE HORSES SMART?

FEI 5* dressage judge Anne Gribbons once told me the perfect horse was the one who was smart enough to know what she wanted and dumb enough to do it.

I can tell you that Arabians and Trakehners are really smart. They are usually a few steps ahead of their riders. Some of the draft breeds or old-style Warmbloods are a bit slower, but also usually a bit safer for beginner riders. Be aware that a really smart horse not only quickly learns good habits, he can quickly learn bad habits, too.

Conditioning can be either the *aid/reward* system or it can be the *ignores the aid/correction* system. Bronze-medal-winning Olympian Carol Lavell once said to me, "One aid, one answer." I agree with her—far too often, we give a multiple-choice test to the horse. Instead, he must be conditioned to react in the right way to our aid, and his reward is that we take the aid off (negative reinforcement). If the horse kicks out at the rider's leg, she should quickly use her leg again or tap with the whip. This should continue until the horse stops kicking, at which point the leg comes off as a reward.

However, the horse kicking at her leg sometimes scares a rider, so she takes her leg off, and the horse learns if he doesn't want to listen to her he can kick and the rider will go away.

A horse learns via logic. His learning is very black and white; there are no gray areas. When the rider does not make a quick correction for a mistake, just continuing on, the horse thinks he did the right thing, and when the rider stops the horse after every mistake, he learns to make errors and just stop—the worst thing he can learn in dressage. Corrections must be quick and fair. The rider must also have enough experience to figure out which aid the horse was incorrectly reacting to. Often inexperienced riders correct a problem with a leg aid or with their reins.

Once the horse has done something correctly, reward him and move on. Don't keep repeating the same exercise until the horse makes a mistake and you have to make another correction. Remember, I keep saying "correction" not "punishment." I believe that if the rider teaches the horse to fight, he quickly learns that fighting is easier than working, and the rider will have created a real and possibly dangerous issue to deal with later.

Sugar is good, and a pat is good as long as it doesn't disturb the contact, and remember your voice can also be used in training to tell the horse he is a "Good boy."

MOVING UP THE LEVELS

As with human students, horses need to be performing at about 64 percent consistently at the highest test of the level before the rider should think about moving the horse up to the next level. The rider also needs to discuss with her trainer the horse's athletic ability and fitness, as well as her own, in order to have a correct influence with her seat and aids.

"CROSSOVER CELLS"

I believe that a horse doesn't have many, if any, "crossover cells." In other words, when he learns shoulder-in *left*, it's reasonable to assume that he would understand shoulder-in *right*. This is not the case, however. It is also why a horse will spook in one direction and not the other. Remember, horses are like us—right- or left-handed—although most of them, like people, are right-handed, which means they are more coordinated on the right, and stronger on the left. So they like to bend right (be short on the right side) and long (or strong) on the left. They usually push into your left leg and want more contact on the left rein. So, as we work to make our horse equal on both sides, we also have to work on our own body to become equal, as we right-handed people will also want to fall to the left when we need strength.

FEAR

Horses can get used to anything. If you don't believe me, watch police-horse training. There is a wonderful class for police horses at the Horse of the Year Show at Wembley in England. Barriers with balloons? Small children leaping about? No problem. I think sometimes that dressage riders don't allow their horses to get used to things—their environment always needs to be too quiet and too still. There is nothing like a few baby carriages or kids playing in a park to get your horse a bit bored with these things. I often say, "Dressage horses may be trained, but they aren't broke." How many of you ever tie your horse to the trailer?

THE VALUE OF A GOOD BREAKFAST

There are many variables with training horses, just like teaching kids in school. Did the kids eat a good breakfast? Did they eat too much sugar? Is the horse being overfed? Does he get turned out? When a horse is underfed, he won't have any energy and won't be able to build muscle, either. Make sure your "student" is healthy and well taken care of, but also has the chance to blow off excess energy so he can concentrate on his lessons. Good stable management is as important as good training, a good vet, and a good farrier. You are all a team!

HOW THE HORSE'S BODY CHANGES THROUGH TRAINING

If the rider and trainer are correctly working the horse, the horse's body will become more beautiful: his topline will develop, the neck will get a lovely "cresty" look, the loins will fill out, and the hindquarters will ripple with muscles. When the horse is being shown at a level that requires collection, he should have the correct muscles to support the collection.

Diagram A shows a topline for a four-year-old that has been started correctly under saddle (note the correct topline beginning). However, he is still a bit long and strung out over the loin, the neck is longer and more level with the ground.

In B we see a seven-year-old horse "on the bit" with a higher and more arched and raised neck and a stronger and shorter loin area.

Diagram C shows a seven-year-old at rest, and therefore not "on the bit" but still showing the nicely developed muscles of the topline.

In D we have an FEI Horse "on the bit" with the neck arched and raised. For me, the poll could be a bit higher, but this drawing shows a horse with a short neck. This type of conformation (or the horse could be a stallion, too) shows how difficult it is to have the poll the highest point and the nose in front of the vertical. As judges, for a "10" we must follow the FEI guidelines and demand both. However, often a horse with a short neck will be "above the bit" if the poll is the highest point. The horse can still get many good marks if the contact is good, the nose is on or in front of the vertical, and the movement is performed correctly with athleticism and correct paces.

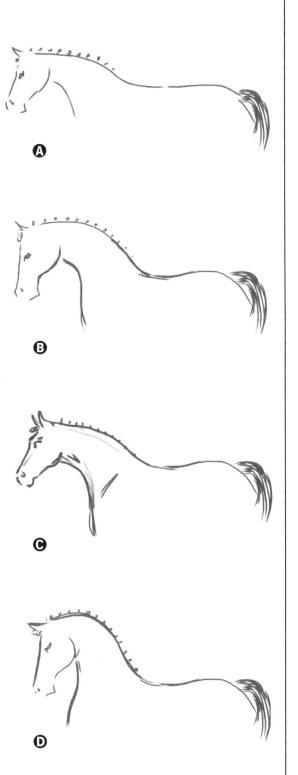

~ PROBLEMS ~
and Solutions

Q Is dressage really for every horse?

A Yes! Dressage is the simplest form of training, and it will benefit any horse. What does dressage do? Keeping it simple, dressage is helping the horse become a more comfortable means of transportation. It will make any horse more rideable.

....

Q How do I get the horse in front of my leg?

A First, see the definition of *putting horse in front of the leg* on page 12. "Chasing" the horse around, with only speed and a strong aid, has nothing to do with what this phrase is about. Your horse needs to have a quick reaction to your leg aid and a quick reaction to your seat aid. Note: a green horse will react 90 percent from the leg and only 10 percent from the seat. With correct training this should change and by the time your horse is starting collection, he should be at least at a 60/40 balance; later at the FEI levels a 10/90.

You need to start early with your horse so he understands he needs to respect your leg and seat. You want him to respond to the lightest possible aid—not you having to use a lot of leg at all times. Think of the lightest aid as a quick squeeze with the calf, or an opening of the seat. When the horse doesn't respond, you need to quickly go to the "more" aid, which is a touch with the spur or a quick kick. Then, if necessary, use the "most" aid, which is using the whip in a tapping motion behind your inside leg.

Q My seat is stuck! I think I use too much leg and my horse is getting dull. When do you start educating the horse about the seat?

A As I mentioned in the last answer, when you first start training a young horse, you need to use 90 percent of your aids from your legs and hands and only 10 percent from your seat. As the horse moves up the levels, this should change and by Grand Prix you would hope to have only 10 percent aids from the leg and hand with the rest coming from the seat. I often find that riders work too hard to *push* the horse out of a gait (or piaffe, in some cases) rather than just allowing him to go forward, and once he is moving forward, to then reinforce the leg aid to increase the power.

Most horses get "stuck" in piaffe, and get more and more frantic because their riders keep adding more and more leg to get them out of it, instead of just *allowing* all that power to go forward by sitting deeper and moving their lower legs more forward and off the horse for a moment.

....

Q "Inside leg to outside rein." Okay, but how? There are many roads that lead to Rome, but without an explanation it's just going to confuse students. It took me until maybe two years ago to get it. If only someone had explained it to me I maybe would have gotten it long ago!

A Trainers need to spend more time talking and explaining things to their students rather than just giving directions like, "More forward," or "More inside leg to outside rein." At the same time, students need to take some responsibility here and not be afraid to ask their instructors when they don't understand. Communication is a two-way street. I always try to tell a new student that she must not be afraid to ask me questions and tell me when she doesn't understand something.

The idea of "inside leg to outside rein" is talking about the horse's balance. Your goal is to gain control of the horse's four legs, which he likes to position like a well-balanced, stable wagon. The horse has stability at the beginning of his training, but not mobility, and in dressage, you want mobility. Another example is that of a roller skate. First, think of the old-style skates with four wheels—one in each corner. Then, think about the inline skates of today with all the wheels on the same track; these have less stability but more mobility, which is exactly what you want as your horse moves up the levels.

So, you need to use *all* of your aids to make this happen, not just the two that are most talked about. To create the "inside-leg-to-outside-rein" feeling on a circle, you need to bend the horse correctly. First, you need your inside rein to move the horse's neck and shoulders slightly to the inside, then the inside leg to push his rib cage outward, followed by your outside leg behind the girth to make sure the haunches do not fall out.

When all this happens, the horse will move the inside hind leg into the space created by your moving his rib cage out: the inside hind leg moves forward and under the body. When the horse has correctly moved the neck and shoulders to the inside, the inside hind leg and outside front leg are now on the same line of travel.

Other ways of saying this: the rider has moved the horse's inside hind leg toward the outside rein, or the horse now stretches into the outside rein by stretching and lengthening the outside of the body. So, if the horse correctly steps toward the outside rein, the rider can use this rein correctly to put the horse more on the bit, and to help transfer a little more weight to the hind legs with a half-halt.

A common misconception is that the outside rein *is* the half-halt. It is only a *part* of the half-halt. When the other pieces do not work, the only thing the outside rein does is to slow the horse down and shorten his neck.

Q **Could you explain how to teach the horse a flying change?**

A This subject takes an entire chapter in my book *Dressage for the Not-So-Perfect Horse*! There is a very clear system in the book. There are many steps and each one needs to be in place before starting the next. You will find some good exercises there, as well as solutions to problems you may encounter.

Q **What are some tips for having your horse stop square when he always wants to step one front foot out?**

A When the horse's front feet are not square, it's possible you have uneven rein contact in the transition. Check to see if you have more weight in the rein that corresponds to the front foot that is out. If so, work with your half-halts to try to get the horse a bit more supple in this rein, and then try the halt again. Be sure you are shortening the trot or canter stride prior to the halt. Horses have difficulty coming to a balanced and square halt from a huge big trot or canter. Narrow the base of support and you should have more success.

....

Q Can any horse collect with correct connection?

A A horse's ability to collect changes, as does his ability to extend, when he is strengthened and gymnasticized. Of course, each horse is an individual so will not have the same results. Horses bred for dressage will develop quicker, while those not bred for the sport will take a bit longer. I never say that any horse will finish at a certain level. I can have my best guess, but often I am surprised and the horse goes a lot further than I thought he could. Sometimes a wonderful work ethic helps out a somewhat limited body!

Think of the developing horse as a beginning figure skater. The first jump he learns is the waltz jump, where he comes forward off one skate, does a small half-turn in the air, and lands. As he develops skill as a skater, coordination as well as physical strength, his jumps will soon involve one full rotation, then two, and if he is really talented, three or even four rotations at the Olympic level. As the number of turns in each jump increases, the speed and height of the jump must also increase.

The best clue is that when the movements are easy to ride, flow nicely, and neither you nor your horse is struggling—then you have the right amount of balance to be where you

are. When not showing in the winter, you shouldn't just concentrate on teaching the horse the new movements needed at the next level, but really take the time to develop the Pendulum of Elasticity (see p. 12) and strengthen his body.

....

Q Do you ask for the canter with the inside leg or the outside leg? Does it depend on the age, training, or discipline?

A When I rode Western Pleasure and the judge stood in the middle of the arena, we only used the outside leg for canter. Actually my horse was so smart, he heard the announcer say, "Lope your horses," and he was off! I think that most hunters are also trained off the outside leg as well.

Remember the left-lead canter starts on the outside (or right) hind. With a green or young horse, I always use more outside leg in the beginning along with my voice. As his training matures, I would add a bit of inside leg at the girth along with a little scooping motion with my inside seat bone. Once the horse knows travers, using too much outside leg can be confusing, so you need to transfer the aid over to the inside leg. Most of my FEI horses would canter off a slight touch with my inside spur at the girth, and from my seat.

....

Q What can you do for a horse that "rope-walks"?

A Some horses are difficult to change very much because of their conformation. A horse that "rope-walks" (a tendency to swing the striding leg around and place it in front of the supporting leg) behind or in front can be helped a bit with shoeing and also lateral suppling exercises, like head-to-the-wall leg-yields or leg-yielding off a straight line. Bending exercises that displace the shoulders a bit and put the inside hind leg more under the horse's body can also be helpful.

Q **Does counter-canter help improve the true canter? Is it a valid training tool or is it just used as a way to train the flying changes?**

A Counter-canter is a great exercise for straightening and strengthening the canter. It also improves the horse's balance—when done correctly. However, in some cases, too much counter-canter can actually be harmful to the changes: when the horse is so comfortable in the counter-canter, he may think twice about wanting to change because counter-canter is too ingrained. So with a well-balanced young horse that shows natural changes, I go ahead and finish the changes before going to the counter-can-ter—although this method won't work with a horse that needs strengthening or balance in the true canter.

Q **Can you outline your groundwork and long-lining protocols for a horse through Third Level? Groundwork is so important, and I do not believe many train-ers spend enough time doing it.**

A I agree and do a lot of groundwork, especially in the beginning. When I backed horses, I would spend 30 days

working with them, then did not mount until they could walk, trot, and canter on the longe line with side-reins, calmly and using the cor-rect muscles (see p. 35). Then, it was easy to mount, get them used to carrying weight on the longe, and go off the longe accepting the bit and using the correct muscles. I do a lot of work in hand with five-year-olds to prepare for the piaffe, and I also do double-longeing and long-lining.

It would take another book to talk about all of it, so I suggest you look for Kathy Connelly's book on long-lining, to be pub-lished by Trafalgar Square Books (www.horse-andriderbooks.com). She is the master!

Q **I love how dressage changes the horse's physique! Why do Upper-Level dressage horses look so different from young horses at Training Level? Their bodies are so beautiful (see sidebar, p. 42).**

A I agree. Olympian Steffen Peters and I love to show this in our symposiums: we have a four-year-old, a Third Level horse, a Small Tour horse, and a Grand Prix horse come into the arena at the same time. It is not only interesting for everyone to see them lined up head to tail, where the development of the muscles is really obvious, but also to see them in motion. Looking at the horses' balance and how their gaits and paces are improved is very interesting, and also a big "Aha!" moment for those who struggle to understand the balance needed at the dif-ferent levels (see the drawings on p. 42 that demonstrate this amazing transformation).

Q Why do people think they have to use a flash noseband on their bridles, and should they be allowed?

A I always used a flash on my horses just to prohibit them from getting their tongues out or crossing their jaws. It is a good tool when used correctly and is not too tight. When applied too tightly, it prevents the horse from chewing the bit correctly, and it can cause resistance.

Q How do you start over after an injury to a horse?

A It's a bit tricky to give advice about starting over after an injury without specific details. I will say that when I had a horse injured, I always gave him two more weeks off in addition to what the vet recommended. Many horses that have been on stall rest are pretty wild when they get to come out and "hand walk quietly." I believe if you are going to hand walk your horse in this situation, a little tranquilizer is not a bad idea for a while. I had one good friend who was very seriously hurt from a hand-walking incident. I am all for wearing a helmet and using a stud chain.

At the end of every show year I always give the horses three weeks off, with just turnout and light trail riding. I think it is good for them mentally, and if there happens to be any little physical problem going on, it sometimes takes care of itself. And, for me the rider, it was good mental relaxation before gearing myself to move up the levels!

Q Why does my horse put her hind legs out behind her and fall on her shoulders? We have less trouble in lateral work than on circles and straight lines.

A You have answered your own question! When you are doing shoulder-in, you have bend: you have the hind legs on the line of travel and the shoulders are displaced in front of the inside hind leg, which allows you to engage it. So, you are losing this line of travel or straightness on the circles and straight lines, which allows the hind legs to escape. Shoulder-in and shoulder-fore are your new best friends. Be aware of keeping the hind legs *on* the line of travel and the shoulders slightly to the inside. This will also keep the horse's belly a bit to the outside, which gives you more room to push the inside hind leg under the body.

Q FEI rules define *on the bit* as "…the head should remain in a steady position, as a rule slightly in front of the vertical, with a supple poll as the highest point of the neck." Why has it become popular to overflex and ride behind the vertical?

A I am not sure that this is a "popular" trend or just a trend that shows the quality of riding needs to be improved. Sometimes, a young horse with a lot of power will come behind the vertical for a few strides as he loses balance. However, I agree with you—I do see way too many horses with short necks and low polls. Many of them are overflexed or behind the vertical due to incorrect use of the double bridle.

PART 2

The Value of the Training Pyramid

CHAPTER FOUR

Balance

This chapter and the next six chapters are devoted to the Training Pyramid (also known as the Training Scale), each discussing an individual element. As you read this book, keep in mind this scale has been around a very long time. It is generally not a good idea to try to jump over any one of the steps. In my lifetime with horses, I have usually found the need to move *down* the scale at times before moving up. Sometimes this was totally to redo a step, sometimes it was for a quick review. I think we all need to think of this Training Pyramid as a two-way highway, and not be afraid to move down to review steps.

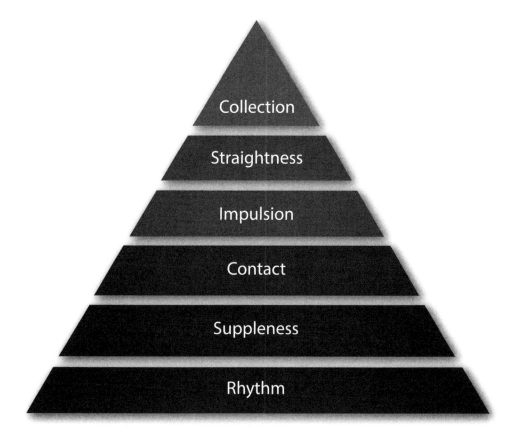

Collection

Straightness

Impulsion

Contact

Suppleness

Rhythm

WHAT IS BALANCE?

There are several issues I need to address before I discuss the Training Pyramid elements one by one. First, I want to discuss the word *balance* in relationship to the levels. When the word *engagement* was kept in the *impulsion* box of the collective marks for the USEF tests at Training and First Level, it wasn't because those levels required the horse to be "weight-bearing." Rather, it was a way for a judge to comment on a horse with a very natural uphill balance at that level.

Training and First Level dressage tests do not require engagement; the horse's balance does not need to be *uphill*. The balance is required to be *level*. Is the Training or First Level horse on the forehand? No, he is in a *level balance*, carrying weight equally on all four legs.

The lengthening at First Level does not need to show an uphill balance, but rather it needs a horse that is strong enough to push with the hind legs a bit more over the ground without becoming irregular or falling on the shoulders. So again, at Training and First Level, the hind legs should push but do not need to carry.

So perhaps you are riding a young overachiever? If your horse does have a natural uphill balance and already shows a talent for some weight bearing on the hind legs, that is okay, too. Judges are trained not to punish you for this. This overachiever might score a "10" on a 20-meter circle, but so could the horse I talked about earlier—the one that is only in a level balance. Do not think that in order to score a "10," you need to ride an overachiever. This is not true. You only need to meet the requirements described in the purpose of each level, and to fulfill the criteria of the movement.

It's Not the Movements, It's the Balance

I think the most misunderstood issue in regard to the levels is that it is *not* the ability of the horse to perform certain movements that makes him a Third Level or FEI horse. It is the *balance* in which he can perform these movements. So, you can have a horse that understands half-pass, or does a flying change, but if he is not engaged and showing a certain amount of cadence and expression in these movements, the score will not be higher than a "5" or "6."

Remember, the balance must be relative to the level. Collection at Second Level will come and go. This is to be expected, as it is early in the horse's stage of development. As the horse progresses up the levels, however, the balance must be more consistent and better maintained. Without the ability to show this, a judge will not be able to reward your performance with more than a "5.5" or a "6." Your score will be in the 58 percent range if you cannot show the balance required in the purpose of the test.

Which Comes First: Lateral Suppleness or Engagement?

In a horse's training early on, I find that I develop these two talents—lateral suppleness and engagement—apart from each other.

My experience has been that without the creation of *lateral* (bending or side to side) suppleness and *longitudinal* (over the topline) suppleness, you as the rider will not have the tools, and your horse will not have the strength, to develop the engagement needed to move up the levels. As I mentioned in the glossary at the beginning of this book, remember what Steffen Peters says, "Suppleness, suppleness, and more suppleness."

The horse's muscles and his body must be gymnasticized and strengthened over the years of training. You can teach the horse the "tricks" or movements, but what creates a true dressage athlete is the correct muscle development of the topline and the loins.

Think about the Training Pyramid. Remember where each step is located in relationship to the others. You cannot create more engagement or better extensions when your horse is crooked, or when he has tension in the topline. You will have to work up and down the scale to correctly train your horse. Don't be stubborn; it is important to be willing to drop down a step or two in the scale and fix the "hole" in the training.

As the horse becomes more mature physically and mentally, the continued strengthening of his body and the increasing amount of suppleness should go hand in hand.

THE FRAME

In a still photo, the horse can be seen in the perfect *frame*—or "pose"—for the upper levels, but it is not until you can see a moving picture that you can really judge if the training has been correct. Just where the neck and poll are positioned is only a small part of the picture.

The frame must be changeable. The rider must be able to lengthen the horse's neck for an extension. If his neck is "stuck," it is not correct dressage.

The joints of the hind legs need to be bending and showing a clear articulation, not only in the air but also in the stance phase of the carrying hind leg. The loins must be raised and the belly muscles in use in order to create elasticity. The horse's back is also the bridge, which carries the energy from the hind legs to the contact. The shoulders must be elevated and lifted so the front legs can show expression and reach and freedom. The horse must spring up in the air and propel himself over the ground in a light-footed, elastic way. His mouth should be closed and softly chewing on the bit, communicating with the rider. There should be no tilting or twisting in the poll.

Ideally, for a "10" score, the poll must be the highest point and the nose should be slightly in front of the vertical. However, as I mentioned in chapter 3 (p. 42), if you look at certain breeds, or stallions, the crest is so big that if the poll were the highest point, the horse would not be on the bit anymore.

The "show frame," which is clearly defined in the FEI Rulebook, and the "training frame" may be different. Each day when you work with your horse, you must ride in the frame that is most productive for training that day. This frame may be deeper and rounder, perhaps, than would be acceptable for a "10" at a horse show. But if your horse is having some tension issues in the topline, you cannot logically get through that with the "perfect" frame. Of course, your goal is to come to the competition with a supple and well-trained horse that can perform for eight minutes the requirements of the test in the correct frame.

DRESSAGE SINS

So, a short neck and a low poll: no more than a "4," correct? No. A judge and a trainer need to have a good eye and the understanding of the training of the horse in order to know how much of a sin is taking place.

Scenario 1: A young horse with a lot of power comes into the rider's hands and gets behind the vertical or the poll gets too low for a few strides. Then the balance is restored and the correct frame is again shown. This is a small mistake, in my opinion. It happens, and if the rider is quick and tactful with the aids, this can be taken care of with a few adjustments and correct half-halts.

What Lightness Really Means

I am just like most of the rest of the dressage world in that at the beginning of my riding, I thought "lightness" referred to how much weight I had in the reins. When I had too much weight, my horse was heavy, and when the contact was very light, almost loose, I really was doing dressage!

I am sure that I was told many times before I actually "heard" it that this wasn't the case; however, sometimes when we are learning, it takes a while for an instructor's words to sink in. Or, perhaps one instructor explains a concept in a different way and you have this amazing "Aha!" moment.

I was also under the impression that if I could just get the horse's hind legs active enough, the forehand would elevate, just like a teeter-totter. So, for the first several years of my dressage riding, I was 100 percent focused on the hind legs. It probably didn't help that I heard "forward and more forward" over and over again from my trainer at the time.

I think the journey today is easier because through biomechanics studies, we have so much more knowledge about how the horse works his muscles. The teeter-totter will not ever work, as the horse's shoulders are not even attached to the rest of his skeleton by bone. So those hind legs can be working like a charm, but the shoulders can still be planted in the dirt!

My first time even *thinking* about the horse's shoulders was in a lesson with a very famous Team rider. While on my horse, she took her outside foot and kicked my horse's shoulder. I was stunned! What was that for? I never really understood what mobility of the shoulders meant before. But that simple gesture pointed out to me how the horse could lean into the shoulders, or even lean into just one shoulder. I had not got the "connection concept" before that.

It was trainer Uwe Steiner who finally got this concept through my thick head. Now, I just want to tell you (so you can understand how dumb I really was), I had already trained two Grand Prix horses by this time. So, Uwe finally says to me, "You must get the shoulders up and more mobile." I stopped and said, "Okay, how do I do that exactly?"

Now remember, I had been training with great people, and I had done very well in the competition ring: I had about 60 percent of this "connection concept" without knowing it, but that last 40 percent of just being able to *think* about moving my horse's shoulders around and keep the *shoulders light* made such a huge difference to my riding—and also to my scores in the ring.

In addition to my horse being in a much better balance, the result was a more supple and elastic contact in the reins. Note, I did not say a "lighter" contact in the reins. That can happen, but with a few of the 17-hand stallions I rode, it did not. However, that's not the point. You need *suppleness* in the contact, and you need *activity* of the hind legs, and you need to work on keeping the shoulders *up* and *mobile*!

Thank you, Uwe and my other great trainers. I am so sorry I was so dense!

Scenario 2: A horse is "curled up" and there is no contact—the reins are actually looping a bit. This is a serious issue. The horse does not have a connection over the back, through the neck, and out to the contact.

Scenario 3: The rider has an unstable position and is balancing on the reins, which cause the horse to shorten the neck and drop the poll. To me, this will give the rider a low score, perhaps a "4," but we need to be fair to the horse, as it is not his fault. So perhaps I'll give a "5" for the submission so I can make a point as a judge that the rider's position is the main problem.

Remember, whether you are a judge, trainer, or a rider, you need to see the whole picture, then notice the small details. Too many in our sport only watch the head and neck and don't pay attention to the whole body of the horse. It requires a good deal of knowledge and experience to know which sin is deadly. The trainer and rider must have a working knowledge of the biomechanics of the horse. Teaching the horse the movements must be coordinated with the gymnasticizing of the horse's physique and by using the Pendulum of Elasticity (see p. 12).

A Rider's AHA! Moment

I tried to use lateral work to help increase my horse's suppleness. However, I found that he responded better to changes within the paces (for example, collected trot to medium trot and back). Then, once he was working well with these transitions, I found his lateral work had improved, too!

Janet says: You will find there is no exact formula when training your horse. You have a lot of tools available, and sometimes you need a simple tool and sometimes a power tool. By using your brain, you were able to approach the lateral-suppleness issue in a creative way! For improved lateral work, don't be afraid to go back to the turn-on-the-forehand sometimes when you need to remind your horse about the simple concept of "move off" my leg! I am glad you felt you were able to experiment a bit and found success.

~ PROBLEMS ~
and Solutions

Q Please explain the importance and meaning of the horse's "frame."

A A *frame* is just a picture in time. The true meaning of "on the bit" is the horse using his muscles correctly within the frame or balance required for the level at which the horse is training. A frame could be a headset, meaning that it might not be adjustable. At the end of the day, correct dressage produces a horse that is very supple and adjustable to the rider's wishes. The rider should be able to make the frame shorter, higher, lower, longer, and the body straighter or bending more quickly when the horse is truly on the aids.

Q I often see horses in a frame that is correct for the level but they still struggle with the movements. Why?

A The horse's frame is only part of the picture—as I said, it is like a still photo. However, dressage must be like a movie, where the horse has correct basics and uses his entire body.

Without good basics, the movements really don't mean anything. I find that if the basics are good the movements take care of themselves. With a new horse, I find it takes a little bit to learn about his reactions and also his personality. There is always a bit of a "dating period" before the real training relationship can begin!

A more average horse will sometimes take two years to move into Third Level and Fourth Level due to the amount of strength it takes for collection and extension. I think there is quite a large jump from Second to Third Level, too.

Q How do we transition our horses up the levels? How much more is needed at each level? Please explain going from Training to First Level. What about the elevation of the withers? Which exercises help this?

A Training and First Level both require the same balance—that is, a *level* balance, which is even weight on all feet. First Level requires a greater degree of "throughness," lateral suppleness, and the horse being on the bit, whereas in Training Level, the horse only needs to *accept* the bit. Elevation in the withers, shoulders, or forehand doesn't come until Second Level when collection is introduced.

Specific "collecting exercises" will help achieve the goal of collection, which includes a better *carrying* hind leg (note: in Training and First Level, the hind legs just *push*, they don't carry). These exercises include shoulder-in, travers, renvers, and half-pass.

Q In working my way up the levels I am having trouble with the balance required from level to level. Is this common? Why am I having so much trouble?

A I remember the first time I took my horses to California to compete and train. I had First Level and Third Level horses, both of which had won everything in my area. I went to the warm-up area and had an "Oh no…" moment, when I saw the other First Level horses. They looked just like my Third Level horse!

It is such a good learning experience to watch a good dressage show, and see how the horses' balance and muscling changes over the course of moving up the levels. An easy way to decide if your horse is ready or not to move up is to ask yourself if you can do the test, and is it *easy*? If you or your horse is struggling, then you are *not* ready. Remember, dressage should look and feel like dancing—not weight lifting.

Q **I want to know how to raise the horse's withers. I read an article about this with Steffen Peters in *Dressage Today* magazine, but I still have no idea how to do it.**

A Yes, Steffen makes it look easy. The elevation of the horse's withers and shoulders or forehand comes with a greater degree of "carrying" in the horse's hind legs, and also correct muscle development of his topline. Since his shoulders are not hung on the skeleton with bone, the horse is not like a teeter-totter or seesaw where the hind end goes down and the other end goes up! Creating this elevation in the forehand takes a lot of timing, along with correct gymnasticizing of the horse's muscles.

Q **What is the perfect frame?**

A As I already mentioned (p. 52) a *frame* (or topline) is only a *part* of the equation. Good riders, trainers and judges all need to look at the *big* picture, notice the whole horse, then look at the small details. The horse is a living and breathing athlete, who has different mental moods, as well. I am sure some days he wakes up tired and crabby and perhaps a bit stiff and sore from the work the day before. What makes dressage so difficult is not having a nice "owner's manual" to tell you which button to push in order to create the same reaction from the horse every day. Riders need to understand that their partner can only be as good as they are. And as in any job or sport, not everyone, equine or human, is cut out to be the next Olympic Gold Medal.

The rider should have reasonable goals about where she wants want to go with her horse. She must endeavor to find the best trainer she can. Learning to ride the *whole* horse with suppleness and impulsion is not always easy.

CHAPTER FIVE

Rhythm
(TAKT)

Maintaining the *rhythm* of the paces is the priority of dressage training. Anytime the training creates rhythm problems, the training is incorrect. I remember a long time ago, Finnish Olympian Kyra Kyrklund said in a symposium, "You can improve the trot the most, improve the canter a little bit, and only ruin the walk." Over the years, I found this to be true.

VOCABULARY

Confusion is often generated by dressage tests, as the rider thinks the word "rhythm" only covers one thing, for example, when the horse is lame, there is no rhythm. Of course, this is not always the case, and to explain, I need to discuss some different words and their meanings.

In the United States, we have a very good judge-training program and were one of the first countries to put a priority on the biomechanics of the horse. The vocabulary taught to American judges is very specific, and oftentimes, judges from other countries are not quite as clear with their words. For example, a foreign judge might just say in the comments, "Horse lost rhythm." An American judge can use a variety of words instead, which mean very specific things. Here are some of them:

Tempo: This is the *repetition* of the rhythm—that is, faster or slower but still in the correct rhythm for the gait. So a judge might say about a trot: "Tempo varies." This means the rider is allowing the horse to go faster, then slower: the rhythm is correct, but its speed is different.

Unlevel Strides: Here the horse has the correct rhythm, but one leg is taking a higher step. For example, in the medium trot, the front legs are not elevated to the same height. Or, perhaps in passage, one hind leg is higher than the other. This term describes the legs when they are in the air.

Uneven Strides: Again, the rhythm is correct, but here, there is one hind leg taking a shorter step than the other. This can occur in walk, especially if there is tension in the horse's back. It is also sometimes seen in trot when there is a pattern of "long" then "short" with the hind legs.

Rhythm Problems: Sometimes a horse trips, or the rider creates a temporary rein lameness (by restricting the horse with one rein), or perhaps the horse hits a deep spot at X. All of these things may cause a few steps of incorrect rhythm, but the problem is not consistent. It will be enough to lower your score, however, depending how pervasive it is throughout the test.

If the trot has 100 percent irregular rhythm, the judge will probably blow the whistle and eliminate you for lameness (see below). Often, a rider cannot feel lameness, and the judge, whose responsibility it to protect the horse, needs to make sure no more harm comes to him by letting the test continue.

Irregular: This comment is used mostly in *trot*, and if the judge sees it consistently in both directions, in all likelihood you will be eliminated. Judges use other terms that will *not* get you eliminated, such as *uneven* and *unlevel* (see above and p. 59). An *irregular* walk is not cause for elimination, but you will not receive a mark higher than a "4" when every step is lateral, which is the most usual problem with the walk. (A *lateral* walk means the horse's legs on the same side of the horse are moving together. Pacing is another term often used for this.) *Uneven* steps at walk can receive a slightly higher score but it's still usually below a "6". Rhythm problems in the walk can lower the gait score in the Collective Marks.

Gait Score

The *Gait Score* in the Collective Marks is a reflection of the rhythm of all the gaits and paces shown and required in the test. This score is also influenced by the freedom and quality of the gaits. A horse with correct rhythm in all three gaits, but with little freedom or elasticity, will have a lower score than a horse with correct rhythm in all three gaits that also shows *reach, freedom, expression*, and *elasticity*. Think of the "wow" factor when you see a horse that just takes your breath away. Correct training and correct muscling of the horse will improve a horse's natural gaits: the trot improves the most, followed by the canter, but the walk you are pretty much stuck with—remember what Kyra Kyrklund said, "You only ruin the walk…."

• STORY FROM THE ROAD •

I AM HERE!

In all of the years of flying, I have always ended up at the correct airport, until a fateful trip in 2014. I had been contacted by "Anne Marie" via a post on Facebook to do a clinic in Quebec. So she and I agreed on a date a year ahead of time. The whole time we "talked" it was to be in Quebec. I agreed to send books up for signing, and she gave her shipping address to my publisher.

So on a Friday I boarded the plane from West Palm Beach, Florida, to Quebec City. I arrived, got through immigration, and stood waiting outside the door of International Arrivals. I did not see anyone with a sign, and Anne Marie had said she would meet me. Hmmm. After about 20 minutes, when the area had cleared, I turned on my iPad (for some reason I had no phone service), and sent a message to Anne Marie. Here is the imessage "conversation" word for word:

AM: I am here when you come through the glass doors in the arrivals area. I will be on your right. I am wearing a grey coat, blond hair with glasses, around 5 feet 9 inches. See you soon.

JF: Do not see you. I have a purple long down coat on with gold purse and blue carry-on.

AM: I am on the right side of the doors. Where are you standing?

JF: I am by a big column to the right of the doors. Are you in a different terminal?

AM: I am at International Arrivals. Do you see the flower shop? Are you inside or outside?

JF: No flower shop here. I am inside. I will ask if there is another arrival area. I came in from Newark on United. It is a small terminal. I am taking a photo of where I am standing. (*I post photo.*)

AM: I am trying to figure out where you are in the airport.

JF: I am going to the information desk.

AM: I am also at the information desk.

JF: Here is a selfie of me and where I am standing. (*I post another photo.*)

The information desk says this is the only arrival area. I am in Quebec City.

AM: Oh no! You are in Quebec City, not in Montreal?

JF: I am in the wrong airport? Did you not see when I sent the reservation to you?

AM: No, you just sent the arrival time. Is there an Air Canada flight to Montreal? There is a flight every hour. Go to the Air Canada desk, they will fix it. I am trying to arrange something.

JF: Bus goes at 7:00 p.m. It is $100 CAD, the air is $471 CAD. I am headed to the bus station. Since I bought the ticket on United, Air Canada won't fix anything. I would have to call United and my phone isn't working.

Continued next page

AM: Go buy the ticket, we will pay.

JF: Okay.

AM: I am talking with an Air Canada supervisor. Give me your booking reference number with United.

JF: Okay, here it is, but it won't do any good. (I send her my reference number.)

AM: Is there a flight leaving soon?

JF: Well the cheapest one leaves at 9:00 p.m. (It is now 5:00 p.m.) I will buy a seat on that one. I will stand by for earlier ones. Will let you know when I board. Gads, so sorry. This has never happened before.

AM: Thumbs up! We will adapt, no worries. Keep me posted. Wanted to bring you out to dinner but we will go straight home.

JF: Okay, I think I will get on the 7:30 p.m. I changed my return ticket on my iPad (cost of $530) so on Sunday we are good to go.

AM: Okay, we will drink a martini or two! LOL.

I get through security and see a flight boarding for Montreal. I tell the nice ticket agent my sad story, and he lets me on the flight. It is now 5:30 p.m. The flight is only 30 minutes, so not too much time lost.

JF: I am here at baggage, Domestic, by the Tim Horton.

AM: Yes, I am here!

And, finally, we meet!

So the moral of the story is to ask specifically which airport to use. Anne Marie explained to me that everyone in Canada says, "Come to Quebec" and never says which city you are supposed to go to! Here in the United States we say, "Come to Houston," not "Come to Texas"! Anyway, lesson learned for both of us!

Most judges will take the three gaits and average them for the final Gait Score. When the *lengthenings, mediums*, and *extensions* show improved freedom, it gives the judge more information and thus an option to move the Gaits Score upward. However, lack of freedom in these movements is not a reason to move the score downward.

Dressage is all about "doing no harm" to the rhythm of the gaits. It is also about improving the *quality and expression of the gaits*. By following the Training Pyramid and correct dressage principles, you will keep on the right track.

~ PROBLEMS ~
and Solutions

Q My Thoroughbred has absolutely the best walk I have ever sat on, and I've only ever seen one I thought looked as good. We waited a very long time to ask for any kind of collected walk, simply because it would have been so easy to mess up when he wasn't strong enough to really hold himself yet! How do I make sure I am able to keep this good walk and the correct rhythm as we train?

A Lucky you for having a good walk on your horse. Too many riders are impatient with the walk and only allow the horse short periods of walk on a long rein between exercises. I have found it very important for the rider to wait until the horse relaxes before picking up the reins again. Otherwise, how will the horse ever learn to do that at the show?

....

Q My trainer says you can ruin the walk. I think people ignore the walk because it's the walk, but they might also be ignoring what they are doing in the saddle at the walk, like fidgeting with the seat and reins. It's at the beginning of the ride so no one is warmed up yet. Are there good pointers about how to keep the lovely walks we have?

A Riders tend to "push" or "drive" too much with their seats at the walk. They need to remember that walk has no impulsion, which means the gait doesn't have a suspension phase, so the use of the driving seat actually ruins a walk. Instead, use clear alternating leg aids and alternating seat aids. Just allow the horse

to move your seat for you. He will rock you a bit from one seat bone to the other. Then feel how his rib cage moves into your lower leg as the ribs move back and forth. When you feel the ribs move into your leg, that is the time to give a quick squeeze—then you are influencing the correct hind leg.

The second factor that causes rhythm problems in the walk is the suppleness of the horse's topline. Any tension in his topline has an immediate effect on the clarity of the rhythm.

I think it is very important for a rider to spend enough time in the free walk so that the horse can relax and breathe. She needs to do this several times during her ride. And, she must be patient and really allow the horse to relax. Otherwise, he will never learn! The rider should also practice many transitions from free walk to medium walk to free walk so he doesn't learn that every time she picks up the reins she is going to ask for trot. This is why so many horses jig whenever the reins are picked up.

AHA! Moment

I heard it said once, "The horse must be more supple through the topline so he can better use his back." I love this description because my "Aha!" moment was when I learned that tight, quick steps are usually caused by a tight back. Relaxation and suppleness equals bigger strides.

Janet says: As you describe it, the horse's muscles are acting just like wires that conduct electricity! (See more on p. 68.)

If you do have some rhythm issues, riding a bit of shoulder-in or renvers also helps. Even a bit of leg-yielding—anything that asks the horse to extend his limbs and take bigger steps and loosen his topline.

Q If I buy a horse with an "8" trot and canter and a lateral walk, can I still do well in the show ring?

A Well, of course, with correct training you can get very high scores with the trot and canter work. However, remember the walk is up to 40 points in the test, maybe more if there are walk pirouettes or turns-on-the-haunches. You will lose marks in these movements, depending on how pervasive the lateral tendency is. A few steps will not be marked down as much as total pacing. Then, if the two walks (depending on the levels—either free and medium or collected and extended) are both problematic, the judge will have to lower the Gait Score as well.

AHA! Moment

My "Aha!" moment came when I was focusing on transitions with the supple back of the horse: not just on the bit, accurate, and with energy, but retaining the swing in the horse's back. It's not easy, since I almost have to "allow" the horse to swing his back and get out of the way myself, not to override, as well as not over-managing during the transition itself.

Janet says: I just love these moments. They keep you coming back for more!

Q Why can't I get high scores with a gaited horse in a dressage show?

A Dressage training and its concepts will help improve any horse; however, in a competitive setting, the correct rhythm of the gaits is the foundation of classical dressage. Since the judge's score starts with the rhythm (is it correct or not?) when the gait is not correct, the score will be no higher than a "5" which is marginal, and possibly, only a "4," which is insufficient.

Q When a judge says "good rhythm" in a test, what does that mean?

A Well, in my opinion, rhythm is either there or not. You either have it or you don't. I think when judges say that, they are really thinking that you have done a good job of maintaining a steady tempo. They just need to improve their vocabulary!

Q Why, when a horse is irregular in trot, will he be eliminated, and yet, when some irregularity shows up in the lateral work, he is allowed to continue?

A If the horse shows a marked lameness on straight lines, it is the judge's duty to eliminate him and protect him from further harm. When there are no rhythm problems on the straight lines and only in the lateral work, this is blamed on lack of lateral suppleness or submission to the bend. The comment usually is "lacking cadence."

Q My horse has a four-beat canter. What can I do to improve this?

A So much depends on the conformation of your horse. A horse with very straight hind legs and not much bending of the joints will be difficult to improve. Usually this issue occurs in horses with little natural suspension. Sometimes, a little jumping will help. The horse learns to "bascule" over the jumps and this will loosen his back, which can help with the suspension.

Q When I buy a new horse, which gait is the most important?

A Buy the best canter you can afford. The trot is the gait you can improve the most with training. The canter you won't change very much, and the walk, as we've said, you can only ruin.

CHAPTER SIX

Suppleness
(LOSGELASSENHEIT)

"**S**uppleness, suppleness, and more suppleness." I use this mantra often in my clinics and symposiums. I guess if someone asked me to use one word to describe what was wrong with dressage training and riding, I would have to say, "Suppleness." A horse is supple when he is loose in the back and he can stretch his neck forward and downward into the contact in all three gaits.

USING THE BODY

For me, this term brings to mind how the horse uses his body: how he uses his topline and also how he uses his abdominal muscles. It is also, along with concept of *contact*, the most difficult thing to learn, feel, and teach. No wonder suppleness is so difficult to accomplish…for riders at *all* levels.

Remember that the most important part of your body in dressage is your brain! Without the mental understanding of what you are trying to accomplish with the horse, you will never "get it." When learning a new sport of any kind, correct reactions take time. Dressage is one sport where our natural instincts are usually wrong. So, the rider must learn to *think* first, then *react*. Only by repeating the correct reactions will the rider become accomplished and skillful.

The rider needs to develop "feel" and technique in order to create true suppleness in the horse. What does suppleness and "throughness" in a horse really mean?

ENERGY SUPERHIGHWAY

Keep thinking of the muscles over the horse's topline as being like a superhighway. When these muscles are supple and loose, a condition that is even required in Training Level tests, the energy (like cars) from the hind legs can travel at full speed with no roadblocks. However, as soon as any tension invades any part of the topline, a "traffic jam" will ensue, and the energy can no longer travel smoothly on the highway.

Another way to think of these muscles is that they are like wires that conduct electricity. The hind legs are the batteries—where *energy* is created in the lower levels of dressage, and stored as engagement in the higher levels. If you screw an imaginary light bulb into the horse's poll and connect the wires, and all of the topline muscles are supple and correctly conducting energy, your light bulb will burn at the same brightness throughout your ride. However, if there is a little short somewhere along the line, the bulb will flicker. These little shorts in the electricity cause a disruption of the energy from the hind legs.

It is a very important concept in dressage to think about the energy or rpms (revolutions per minute) that are coming through the horse. A rider should be able to "feel" an extension or "feel" a canter pirouette *now*! It is wrong to think that you need to create more rpms for an extension because these revolutions should be at the same level throughout your ride. Then you can just adjust them to cover more ground or collect a bit more.

So, suppleness is creating a supple and elastic pathway for the energy from the hind legs to flow smoothly over the back, through the neck and into the contact. Then, when the contact is also supple and elastic, you have the ability to half-halt this energy and send it back to the hind legs through the horse's abdominal muscles (see Circle of Energy, below). As the loin and back lift, so do the abdominal muscles that pull the hind legs more under the body. Physically, when the back is pushed down, the belly also goes downward. Then the hind legs cannot work as we need them to do in dressage. Instead, they "push out" behind the horse, which only serves to put the horse more onto his shoulders.

When you wonder if your horse is supple, "through," and connected, you must ask yourself the questions about the correct flow of energy from, and back to, the hind legs. Do you have deviations or traffic accidents? Or a flickering light bulb? This concept is often called the "Circle of Energy" or the "Circle of the Aids." The rider's calf sends an aid through the abdominal muscles to the "battery" (the hind legs), where the energy is created, that takes energy over the "power lines" (the supple muscles of the back and neck) to the "light bulb" (contact). This energy then travels up the reins through the rider's arms and back down through the rider's body to the calf where the process begins again.

~ PROBLEMS ~
and Solutions

Q **Many times we can supple horses in the poll and jaw or even in the hind end, but I find the middle of the horse, especially where the saddle fits, the hardest to supple. What are the best exercises?**

A Moving that "dining car" out of the way takes some work! Remember the image of the horse as a little three-car "choo-choo" train (with the cars' hinges in front of the saddle and behind it—see p. 6). So on a circle, the shoulder-and-neck "car" needs to come in as the "dining car" (saddle area) is pushed out, and the "caboose" (hind end) comes in, too.

One of my favorite exercises is going onto a 20-meter circle with a lot of inside bend, then counter-bending and leg-yielding down to a smaller circle (decreasing the size of the circle). Change the bend to suit the smaller circle and then leg-yield back out to the larger circle (increasing the size of the circle). This exercise is also called "Increase and Decrease the Circle." The important aspect is that when leg-yielding back out, you keep turning the shoulder-and-neck car inward, so only the "dining car" and "caboose" move out first; otherwise the horse falls onto the outside shoulder.

• STORY FROM THE ROAD •

KEEP THE LIGHT BULB BURNING!

To finally feel a really well-trained horse connected over the back into a supple contact is an amazing experience. I am not sure I would have had this experience and feeling and been able to put it into my riding without Dennis Callin. Denny is an amazing rider: very natural on a horse, and I think, born sitting up there looking beautiful. He is such a natural rider that back then (remember the 1980s?), it was hard for him to tell someone how to do it. It all came too naturally to him.

He was kind enough to let me ride his amazing Swedish horse Zenith with whom he was long-listed for the US Team. I was struggling with timing on one-tempi changes, so Zenith became my school-master for a few lessons. Well, I did learn the timing on the one-tempis—although it took a while to get 15—and I thought Denny was going to kill me for ruining Zenith's training!

But the real lesson I learned that day was the "feel" of a really well-connected horse. We talk about the "Circle of Energy" and how the electricity comes from the hind legs, over a supple back, through the neck into an elastic contact, lights up the "light bulb" between the horse's ears, and goes back through the abdominal muscles to the hind legs. But until you really feel this, it is a hard concept to get. Lucky for me, I had this amazing chance to ride Zenith. And then, even luckier for me too, I could carry that feeling over to my other horses.

Q I always struggle on my horse to add power without losing suppleness. I can easily get suppleness when in the working gaits, but once more power is added with collection or extension, the suppleness always suffers. What do you suggest?

A Join the club! Suppleness comes before engagement and impulsion, and the more impulsion you have, the more submission you need!

Q What is the relationship between lateral suppleness and longitudinal suppleness?

A A horse can be supple to the bend (with *lateral* suppleness) but at the same time, not be on the bit (lacking *longitudinal* suppleness). A horse can bend and still have his neck quite high and stiff. He can also be "round" through the topline but not able to bend laterally. So for a horse to be considered

totally "through" and on the aids, he has to be laterally *and* longitudinally supple. In my opinion, the half-halt doesn't work when the horse is not submissive to both kinds of suppleness. So, the horse does not have longitudinal suppleness if he is not on the bit.

Q Where does suppleness come from? Am I to feel this in my hands? My seat? The horse's spine?

A The suppleness that comes from the horse allows us to have access to all of his "good" muscles. You can then conduct the electricity the hind legs create over a supple topline. You should feel a swinging back under your seat, and you feel an elastic contact with your hands. The horse's spine is bone so cannot be supple—I'm only talking about soft tissue.

Q Many times I see riders pulling and holding their horses' heads to their knees with only contact on the bending rein—all in the name of "suppleness." Can you can help them understand that the horse is not becoming suppler with that method? And that suppleness is not about making a "rubbery" neck?

A You are right. It is not a good idea to teach the horse to separate his neck from the shoulders. When a horse is more advanced, he does need to learn about the inside rein as a bending (turning) rein and he should yield easily to this aid, just as he would turn his neck for a piece of sugar given him from the saddle.

AHA! Moment

Suppleness and relaxation are inversely related to stiffness and tension. Stiffness and tension can be caused by a ton of things but one to think about: you musn't get upset when you hit a "roadblock" because that alone can make tension worse.

Janet says: So true! The horse needs mental relaxation and the right amount of tension in the muscles for the correct work. Rigid tension is never correct!

Q **Don't you think it is important to explain that lateral suppleness and flexion come before vertical softness? And what about suppling the poll?**

A Bending will help the horse relax and stretch one side of his body, which often helps him relax his topline. Sometimes, however, as there is no magic formula, you need to get the longitudinal suppleness first and then add the bending.

Q **"Poll-flipping" (poll-suppling)— when and how can it be done?**

A The horse has long muscles in the neck, along the vertebrae. These muscles are developed with correct training, giving the FEI Level horse a "cresty" look. When the horse is supple laterally in the neck and poll, you will see these muscles "roll" back and forth over the vertebrae as the bend is changed. This is often described as "flipping the poll."

Sometimes, the muscles get "stuck" near the horse's poll. When this happens, we say the horse is not supple laterally in the poll. It happens usually to the left. When the poll is not supple you see the horse's ears tilting and oftentimes see or feel some tension in the mouth, as well.

Supling the poll can be done with "crest-flipping" or "poll-suppling" exercises. This step is the final part of your lateral suppleness work and will be important for collected lateral work. Note: The base of the neck is naturally very supple and it is very easy to separate the neck from the withers, and this is a mistake. You need to make sure

the poll is letting loose and moving, not just the neck from the base.

As to *when* suppling the poll can happen, I feel as soon as the horse has accepted the contact in both reins. There is a detailed piece about suppling the poll along with exercises and helpful photographs in my book *Dressage for the Not-So-Perfect Horse.*

Q **I never knew about "poll-flipping" until a couple of years ago. Where do you see poll suppleness causing problems?**

A I still see way too many horses in the Prix St. Georges classes that are tilted and stiff in the poll to one side. Riders need to work on this poll suppleness for a long time before they get to the FEI levels—perhaps *as soon* as the horse has accepted equal contact in both reins!

Q **Is drilling "poll flips" counterproductive?**

A *Anything* that is "drilled" will make the horse dull and is counterproductive!

Q **I was taught about "poll-flipping" right away when I started my horse. Why was I told to do it first at the halt?**

A It is important that the rider understands how to do poll-suppling exercises and *why* they do it. Anything new for horse or rider should be done in halt or walk before attempting it at other gaits.

Q I was once taught that every horse starts off with a stiff and supple side. When you warm up the easier direction first, your horse will find the stiff side far easier to warm up. I also learned a lot of shortening and lengthening the stride in the walk at unexpected places, and off my seat, gets my horse's whole body more supple and, therefore, more forward and in front of my leg. What do you think of this?

A This doesn't always work, but I always think it is easier to start with something the horse likes and is good at before I deal with the more difficult issues. Therefore, warming up in the easier direction first does have some sense to it. We need to keep pecking away at the difficulties but we should not overwhelm the horse with our requests. Little discussions and then back to the horse's comfort zone!

> ## AHA! Moment
>
> *When in a clinic, I was able to get that "supple feeling" in half-pass because my instructor (you!) helped me figure out how to take the half-halt from the inside leg, outer rein through the horse, to the inner hind! I felt my horse lift his shoulders and just float sideways and forward, staying supple through his body.*
>
> **Janet says:** I think riders spend so long in half-pass riding the horse sideways off the outside leg that they forget about the cadence and engagement that is produced by the inside leg and outside rein!

Q I have a 21-year-old Dutch Warmblood that locks his jaw and will not round his frame. What kinds of exercises will help correct this? He is sound, in excellent condition, gets chiropractic, and is given supplements. He was a pasture pet from 14 to 16 years old, but now has an excellent work ethic. I think it is more of a habit. He is not in pain.

A It does sound like a habit and that takes a while to overcome. If his teeth are is good shape and his jaw is normal—like humans, as horses age, the conformation of the mouth changes, too—I would suggest changing his frame a lot. Sometimes putting him a bit lower and deeper makes it easier for him to use his back and soften in the poll and jaw. Often, it is the poll that is stiff. See the questions about "poll-flipping" on page 71 and refer to the section on poll-suppling in my book *Dressage for the Not-So-Perfect Horse.*

Q When does physical and mental tension create training issues for my horse?

A Mental tension is a bad thing for dressage, for sure. The horse needs to be confident and attentive to the rider. The muscles of the horse and rider need to have a certain amount of supple tension in them, however. I like to be able to talk about the two kinds of tension— the good and the bad! When the horse has too much mental tension, he will be unable to concentrate on the rider's aids. Physical tension in the topline will create crookedness and a stiff contact. Sometimes you may have both: then it may be time to go for a trail ride or longe him!

....

Q **My frustration with suppleness is: how can I retain it in the busy warm-up arena when I get run down or brushed closely by other riders? How do I maintain it in the "spooky" show arena during windy, stormy weather? It's a whole different ball game out there than it is at home.**

A At a show, I often rode my horses early in the morning when it was quiet, then only 20 minutes prior to the test when things are crazy. However, horses are adaptable, too, and they do get used to bigger venues. Check your nerves and make sure *you* are not the one communicating anxiety to him.

....

Q **At what point in developing supple-ness do you stop blaming training and start looking into potential underlying physiological problems? I have a horse that has a strange twitch, and I can't get rid of it. He has good days and bad days.**

A I think now is the time to call the vet and have a complete workup done. It sounds as if you are making progress, but it is strange that this twitch is still there. Could he have a pinched nerve? If he did not express the behavior when you first bought him, I always suggest you call the vet when a horse changes his personality or way of going in a resistant or weird way. It's best to rule out medical issues and when there are none, *then* you can consider it a training problem.

Q **In your experience, does teeth-grinding always accompany tension? My mare seems to have the best connection when she grinds. When she isn't grinding, the contact does not seem to be consis-tently "through" and she chomps on the bit (you can hear her teeth click quietly—open and closed—in rhythm during the trot). It is almost like she is saying, "I am thinking." She has no ulcers or dental issues.**

A As judges, we are trained to look for more than one sign of tension—like, for example, teeth-grinding plus a wringing tail. Mares are often very sensitive and will do what you describe. I don't think it sounds like tension, although if it does increase a little when you do something harder and decrease a bit when you do something easier, that might indicate tension. But if all is as you describe, I would not worry about it at this point.

....

Q **How do you correct a head tilt going to the left? My 13-year-old mare tilts at the poll and besides wanting to know how to help her, I'd like to know why she does it and if she's uncomfortable.**

A This is a lateral suppleness issue. Typically, horses are stiff in one direction. Think of them as being right- or left-handed. Most horses are right-handed, meaning they like to bend to the right. So, your horse would probably not tilt when going right, as she likes to shorten the right side of her body and stretch the left side.

As I mentioned earlier, the poll is usually the last place to get supple. So, you may have done a good job getting her to bend left, but she still may be stiff in the poll. The tilting shows you she is uncomfortable going in that direction. When you work on suppling (see poll-suppling, p. 71), you can fix this in a fairly short time!

Q Can you explain how suppleness and relaxation only truly come when the horse accepts the connection in the bit, then steps under and rounds up his back? It has taken me way too long to understand this one. Trying to "relax" him too much before asking for connection to the hind legs only succeeds in putting him on his forehand.

A One of my pet peeves is when the word "relaxation" is related to the body of the horse because a relaxed muscle cannot work. So there must be some degree of tension in the muscle—that is, *supple* tension not *rigid* tension!

Q How does the rider know when the horse has become supple and relaxed?

A In sticking with my theme of "keeping it simple," I would say that you will know it when dressage for you means "comfortable transportation." The movements look and feel easy and effortless.

Q I understand that achieving success at the second level of the Training Pyramid should be evidenced by the "swinging back" of the horse. Can you explain what the rider should be "feeling" at this point and offer a detailed explanation of how to "go with the movement" without becoming an obstacle for the horse to balance, or a challenge to the horse's confidence to move so freely?

A For me, a supple back is like sitting on a trampoline or a waterbed. The horse's back will rise and fall as the horse moves, giving the rider a wonderful place to sit. A horse that is stiff in the back will have a jarring gait, and even the best riders will find it difficult to sit. A supple back will suck you down into the saddle a bit, whereas a stiff one throws you up in the air.

Q What tips and guidelines can you suggest for achieving relaxation with higher strung horses?

A At its most fundamental: lots of turnout, exercise, and a good feeding program are all very helpful.

Q I tend to cause my horse's tension by being tense myself in new situations. I understand that I need to remember to breathe. Any other relaxation techniques for the rider to help the horse?

A I found riding to lovely, relaxing, classical music helped me. And a visit to a sports psychologist could help you, too!

Q I have a very flexible, relaxed horse that my trainer has dubbed the "Gumby" horse. I realize this is the opposite of the typical problem but it presents its own challenges because flexible and supple do not necessarily equate, and we lose relaxation when I ask him to carry himself better and not to overbend.

A Well, as I have said many times there is no perfect horse. However, I love ones like yours—they are a challenge but so worth it in the long run!

Stiff horses challenge you with lateral work, but are easier on straight lines; horses like yours are easy to bend and go sideways, but always a challenge on the straight lines. Both types are difficult in their own way, but horses like yours are easier at the end of the day.

....

Q What is the difference between suppleness in a lower-level horse that is in a level balance, and suppleness when a horse is carrying more weight and is more collected?

A As a horse progresses in training, he will have more lateral suppleness than is needed. Think of the transition from leg-yield to half-pass; then think of the progression of the angles in the half-passes. They are very steep at Grand Prix. Longitudinal suppleness must also increase, and the horse must show a very elastic and adjustable topline: piaffe to extended trot for example, or extended canter to a canter pirouette.

Q I know of a trainer who misunderstood "supple" and "contact" to mean you rip the bridle around until the horse is forced to "give" in the neck. How does this affect the flow of energy?

A This sounds like the trainer is merely teaching the horse to separate the neck from the shoulders, which is never a good idea (see p. 70). Remember, the horse must be able to bend like the three-car "choo choo" train with hinges in front of the saddle and behind the saddle (see p. 6). If the energy

AHA! Moment
....

My moment was actually when I got home after a lesson. Suppleness for me was easy to develop when I understood that it needs to be done on the straight line. This was accomplished with little micro-checks in flexion while traveling straight (and later on a circle) to keep the poll soft. When the poll gets soft, so will the jaw, followed by the neck and the back. I think most of us are taught to think of softening the jaw, then we get stuck, literally and figuratively.

Janet says: I do think that when riders talk about the jaw being stiff, it is usually the poll and has nothing to do with the jaw. I also think the poll (laterally) is the last place to be equally supple in both directions. A good instructor will be able to see which part of the horse is carrying the tension and be able to work with the rider with some exercises designed to supple that part.

doesn't travel from the hind legs over the topline and through the neck to the bridle because the rider has separated the neck from the shoulders, then the energy will be grounded down into the shoulders, thus putting the horse more on the forehand.

Q **I would like to see more discussions about suppleness in the rider. At what point between being very supple and too much rigidity (which would be transferred to the horse) is best? How much tension do we need?**

A You are correct that riding is not an exact science. I tell my students to think of tension in their muscles on a scale from zero to 10—with zero equal to sleeping on the couch and 10 being so chock full of rigid tension in their body, they are "frozen." I think that if you reach 10 and hold your breath then start to slowly breathe out and relax down to about 6 or 7, you will have the right amount of tension to ride. You may need to go up to 8 for a half-halt when the horse isn't listening, but if you go down to a 4 or 5, you will be too loose in the saddle.

Q **I have a mare, yes a mare, with a gigantic thick neck (I bet she has an overabundance of testosterone). I see comments about circles and other exercises to attain suppleness. While I totally agree that exercises really are important in the long run to get suppleness, I really think in my case I need a little extra "helping hand." Yes, I am talking about the scary, feared, and dreaded "hand." When**

my horse doesn't start with a soft jowl, we can go around the arena forever and not ever get her over her back. So, I move forward with leg and seat, but at the same time I soften with my fingers and even my wrist. And occasionally, I even bring my hand out and in front to encourage her to drop on the contact that's "sticky" (sometimes I do counterflexions, too).

All the while I am transitioning, forward, back, circles, halts, and even a rein-back and passage! All these things combined get my huge-necked mare supple and ready to do more lateral moves. It's a combination of aids (in my opinion) that bring suppleness and "throughness" and that wonderful feeling when your horse's back is rounded up and under you.

My question is why do people avoid talking about the hand? Rein aids? I really get that we have to ride back to front, but without the half-halt (which is assisted with the reins) and softening with fingers and wrist, you wouldn't have back-to-front riding. So why do so many people seem afraid to discuss the rein aids?

A You will read a lot about the rein aids in this book. You can't ride without them. The leg aids are also discussed, as are the seat aids. At the end of the day, we only have three aids with which to ride dressage: your legs, your hands, and your seat. (You can't really count your voice.) The key is that *all these aids work together* to create a supple and elastic horse. It is when *one* aid takes over and becomes dominant that you are on the wrong path.

Q **I'd like a discussion about the different techniques and exercises for achieving suppleness in different parts of the horse. How do you get "that last piece" of suppleness, which for my horse is the poll?**

A All lateral work supples different parts of the horse. The simple turn-on-the-forehand works at teaching the horse to cross the inside hind leg in front of the outside hind leg; the head-to-the-wall leg-yield teaches the horse to cross the outside hind leg in front of the inside hind. Then you add bend for the travers and half-pass, which stretch the soft tissue across the outside part of the horse's ribs, shoulders, and hindquarters. Shoulder-in helps supple his shoulders. For more on poll-suppling, see page 71.

Q **Will riding back-to-front by engaging the horse's hind legs between a steady contact bring suppleness—when ridden properly?**

A It's the "ridden properly" that gets us sometimes! It is amazing when a rider gets the correct feeling, and the big smile comes across the face! I love those moments when I teach. And yes, if you ride the horse correctly, using the Training Pyramid, you will feel the true suppleness and mobility of your horse.

CHAPTER SEVEN

Contact
(AHLEHNUG)

This chapter deals with one of the most difficult concepts to understand, feel, teach, and learn: *contact*. How much contact is too much and how much is too little? When is the horse too heavy? When is the horse behind the bit (or dropping the contact with the bit)?

LEAN ON ME

The German word *ahlehnug* is a verb which means "to lean on." Interesting that the first piece the horse must learn is to lean on the bit or to take a contact. "Leaning" here does not mean pulling down into the bit or pulling down onto the shoulders. I remember hearing many times from the Masters, "A horse must be heavy before he can be light." Again, we must always remember that lightness is referring to the balance of the horse and the mobility of the shoulders. The contact should be elastic no matter at what level you are riding.

AN ISSUE OF WEIGHT

I believe that all horses are individuals, and to make them happy, they all need differing amounts of contact. The rider, however, needs to be in charge of how much contact is needed. She must create suppleness and elasticity with the contact, and here lies the problem. Contact would be easy to teach if I could tell my student riding, for example, an Arabian (or a Trakehner), "He usually likes a bit lighter contact, so go ahead and take 2 pounds of weight in each rein and hold it." Or, "This Holsteiner stallion likes a bit more contact, so go ahead and take 4 pounds in each rein and hold it."

Contact is really talking about the mouth of the horse and the hands of the rider. How much weight does the rider have in the reins? How much weight does the horse have on the bit? It is wrong for the rider to "hold the horse" up, and it is wrong for the horse to lean on the bit or rest on the rider's hands. The term "connection" refers to the entire horse, as does the word "throughness." For connection and throughness to be established, the hind legs must be active. The horse's back

THE STIRRUP AND STIRRUP LEATHER STORY

Sometimes I take both stirrups and their leathers off a saddle. I keep the leathers buckled and lay them over the top rail of a fence line, with the stirrup irons dangling on the opposite side. I give the rider the ends of the loops of the leathers, one for each hand. I tell the rider to pretend the stirrups are the horse's mouth. Then I say, "Now take hard on one rein." The rider realizes that if she does, the stirrup iron will flip over the top rail of the fence and hit her in the head! You never want to have that much contact with the horse's mouth.

Then I ask her to work with softly moving the stirrup irons up and down, alternately pulling on the leathers to lift the irons and relaxing the pressure on the leathers, which lowers the irons as the leathers slide smoothly over the rail. Consequently, there is not more contact when she takes a little nor is there no contact when she gives a little.

I want her to think of the weight of the stirrup irons in her hands as the weight she has in her hands when she has contact with the horse's mouth. She should softly bend and unbend her elbows in order to move the irons a bit up and down, and it should feel similar to what it's like to follow the contact with the horse.

muscles must be supple and swinging. And the rider and horse must have an elastic and communicative contact between them.

However, it is not that simple. First of all, the weight of the contact will change, or ebb and flow, so to speak. If a horse is falling heavily on his shoulders, you will feel more weight in the reins. If he is reluctant to bend, or shorten one side of the body, you will feel more weight and more resistance in that rein. Then on the hollow side, where the horse likes to bend, the rein will be very light, as the horse doesn't want to have contact there. Most horses have one rein they like to lean on a bit, and one where they don't want to take contact. This has to do with whichever side of the horse is stiff. The long side of the horse will stretch into the contact and the short side will not, and it is that side where you have the light rein.

FEEL AND TIMING

It all comes down to *feel* and *timing*: two things that are hard to teach, and harder yet to learn. It is the rider's duty to make sure the horse becomes equally supple in both directions, so that he can have equal weight in both reins. Without this, the horse will never develop true self-carriage.

A horse is not "light" just because the rider has no contact. The horse is light when the hind legs are carrying weight—not just pushing—and he has developed an increased mobility of the shoulders or the forehand. The rider must be able to give both reins, and I mean *really give*—a loop in both—in order to test this self-carriage. Often, I say to my students that they are not *really* giving the reins, they just aren't pulling as hard! Being able to test the horse to see if he is supple in both reins is very important, because if the rider can't test the horse, the horse will test the rider.

Let's go back for a moment to *suppleness* (p. 67). What does this mean? I like a horse with a supple contact because that is the horse that will have a good conversation with me. I can play a bit with one rein, and the horse will chew back softly in response, or perhaps yield a bit more in the poll, either laterally or longitudinally, depending on which rein I use (see chapter 3, p. 35). When the horse communicates back to me responding to my aids, I will reward that response with a lightening of that aid, a small movement with the rein toward his mouth, or a "give" or softening.

I see many riders just "throwing away" the reins for no reason. Remember, you must have a *reason* to give…and you must create that reason. Your aids must be clear to the horse, then he will yield and respond, and you can give or reward him. This is timing. This is feel.

A rein contact that is pulling or is non-elastic is bad. But so is a rein contact that is constantly looping and losing contact with the mouth. It should go without saying, but since I see too many unstable seats in the show arena, it needs to be said again: without a stable seat you will never be able to have a sympathetic, elastic, feeling contact with the horse because you will be also using the reins as a way to hold on and to stabilize your position. Get longe lessons!

THE BABY BIRDS

Many trainers tell riders to move their fingers. I have very small hands and have always found this causes too much of an open hand for me, and thus a loss of contact and rein length. So I tell the "baby bird" story:

If you were to capture a baby bird in your hand, you would hold it softly with closed fingers. Too open a hand will allow the bird to escape and too much squeezing will kill the bird! This is a good visual for the rider, and plus, when teaching I can call out, "Your baby birds are escaping," or "Stop murdering those poor baby birds!"

BITS, NOSEBANDS, AND OTHER GADGETS

Finding the right bit for your horse is important in developing a good contact. Horses that are a tad nervous in the mouth do well with a fixed ring bit, or perhaps a Mullen mouth bit. These bits allow you to have a more stable contact because this "busy" type of horse often drops the bit. On the other hand, a horse that is less busy and "chewy" will need some help to get the saliva going. Feeding him sugar before riding can start the saliva, and a loose-ring snaffle is best. With the loose ring, you will get more play out of the bit with your rein aids. This type of horse often wants to lean on the bit.

Most trainers have a "bit drawer" full of different types. Borrow some and experiment until you find the right fit for your horse. Sometimes, you will need to change the type of bit after a few months. Make sure you consider the size of your horse's mouth—for example, a horse with a small mouth will not do well with a very thick bit. Also, the nerves of the horse's mouth are in the corners of the lips. A snaffle is supposed to work on the corners of the lips. You need to adjust the snaffle with several wrinkles, as the middle of the bit hangs lower than the rings. If the bit is

THE FISHING STORY

I believe *contact* is one of the hardest concepts to understand. It is trying to teach and learn a "feeling." This type of concept is not concrete, so it is very difficult from both the learning and the teaching end. See if this story helps you understand what a correct and supple contact should feel like.

In Colorado, we do a lot of fly fishing. We stand in the middle of a river or stream, which has a gentle current. We cast, trying to make the trout think we are little flies on top of or in the water, perfect for eating. Once we have the fish on the hook, however, we very gently begin to reel it in. If we pull on the line too hard, we lose our fish. The little bit of "taking" we do in dressage is like this feeling we have on our fishing line.

Then we should also be able to let a little line out and allow the current to take the fish softly away from us, and be able to bring the fish back to us again with a bit of gentle taking on the line. This is the give and take of correct contact. Let's say that your trout was not a trout after all, but rather a 15-pound bass, and it has taken the fly and dived to the bottom of the stream or lake. This is equivalent to the horse that is not respectful of the rider or the *contact*.

too low, not only can the horse can get his tongue over it, but when you take and release contact with the reins, the middle of the bit lifts slightly upward, then falls down on the horse's teeth or tongue.

Using a double bridle should not be an option until your horse is supple and submissive in a snaffle. The double is a *refinement* of the aids.

I like a padded noseband with a flash attachment. I find it hard to get a good fit with a drop noseband. I believe in not allowing the horse to learn to open his mouth and get fussy with his tongue. As mentioned earlier in the book (see p. 47), you don't want to have the flash attachment too tight, as the horse needs room to move his jaw and chew the bit. The new Micklem noseband can be helpful for certain horses (www.williammicklem.com). Don't be afraid to experiment and see what works best for your horse.

Using a running martingale with a young horse is not a bad idea if he likes to throw his head up into your face. The martingale should be adjusted so it only comes into play when the horse is being resistant. Draw-reins are also helpful in the *right hands* but a disaster in the wrong hands. Be sure to work with your trainer to find the right combination of bits, nosebands, and gadgets.

SHAKING HANDS

Think about meeting new people. There are three types of handshakes:

1. The first one is the soft and fingertip-only type of shake. Very wimpy in my opinion—it doesn't give us the feeling of a confident person.
2. Then there is the total put-you-to-your-knees type of hand-shaker. This person is showing dominance, is too strong, and squeezes your hand until it hurts.
3. Then, the perfect handshake comes along. The hand closes softly but firmly around your hand, and the shake is not violently up and down, rather a soft undulation through the nicely bent elbow in a gentle give and take.

The third handshake is how you want to communicate with your horse. Neither of the first two methods will do!

~ PROBLEMS ~
and Solutions

Q I think contact and connection are the hardest of the Training Pyramid elements to learn. How do you follow the horse's mouth while maintaining the appropriate level of connection—not pushing the horse forward into an unyielding hand? I also have a hard time with self-carriage and how to get it!

A The contact must be elastic, like a rubber band. You need to use the soft bend in your elbows to be able to give or perhaps take a bit more contact. You never want the reins having a huge loop in them or being so tight that the horse's neck gets short. The horse should never take the bit like a fish taking a fly and dive to the deepest part of the river—you should be able to gently reel him in (see p. 82). Nor should the horse drop the contact and hide from the bit. Finding the right amount of contact with each horse is a skill that is developed with practice and experience. As mentioned, a good seat and stable position is a must for this to happen. You should be able to half-halt and then lighten the contact (unbend your elbows a bit—think of pushing the horse's nose more in front of the vertical with the reins) as a reward for the horse. This is necessary to improve self-carriage, too.

Self-carriage is something that comes and goes. The rider wants it…the horse not so much. The rider's timing and ability to quickly discover where the horse is cheating is important. I often say to my students, "I have never written on a dressage test that a rider has done too many half-halts." I have written, however, that the rider could make *more effective* half-halts.

The horse can only be in self-carriage when these other pieces are in place:

1. An active hind leg.
2. A supple topline to carry the energy to the contact.
3. An elastic and even contact with the bit.
4. Straightness.

Q I'm just now grasping the concept of connection and contact, but I have a feeling there is much more that I'm not even aware of. Please help.

A Contact and connection are very hard to learn and hard to teach. So you are not alone! And to make it more confusing, every horse is a bit different in the amount of contact he needs or will accept. At the end of the day, sometimes it feels like dressage is a bit like a big science project—we are always experimenting.

Q I am confused about the outside rein. I come from a hunter background and this is not a concept we use. Can you help me understand the proper use of this aid?

A I think that there is an incorrect overuse of the outside rein in dressage. Many trainers and riders seem to think it is the biggest part of the half-halt, which it is not; it is merely the final part. And without the horse having a supple back and neck, the outside rein won't work in a half-halt anyway! I hope that when you read about the rein aids, what each one accomplishes, and how the legs and seat work with the two reins, your understanding of the job of the outside rein will be more clear to you! There is a very detailed discussion about the rein aids in *Dressage for the Not-So-Perfect Horse*.

Q How can I achieve the best, constant connection?

A No one is able to create a correct contact without a correct and independent seat. So even though contact is about the hands, the priority should be the seat! Once riders have good seats, are balanced over their lower legs, and don't need the reins for balance or support, then the true journey of communicating with their horse through the rein aids will be much easier.

Q How important is the outside rein? Then, what is truly connected and forward?

A As I just emphasized on p. 84, the outside rein is often mentioned as the most important aid in dressage, which it is *not*. It is one part of the aids that we need to use in harmony in order to create back-to-front, supple riding. The outside rein controls the speed and also the length and height of the neck. However, the outside rein must work with the inside rein, as well as the rider's leg aids, in order to be effective.

For me, a horse that is truly connected and forward is a horse that doesn't have to be driven every stride by the rider, and one that has enough balance on his own to not lean on the reins. This horse should be able to perform the exercises with harmony and ease.

Q The biggest problem I see is getting the horse to understand the use of the outside rein. How can I help my horse understand this concept?

A I disagree with your statement in one aspect. I think the horse is not the problem. Frequently, the rider doesn't understand how the outside rein works in harmony with the other aids. Riders like to make it the most important aid, and I'll say it again, *it is not*.

Q Help my connection and "throughness"!

A *Connection* and "*throughness*" are terms used a lot but not understood very well. Remember to think of your horse as a science project: The hind legs are the batteries. The muscles that run through his back and neck are like the wires that connect those batteries to the bit. This current should flow equally and smoothly from the hind legs, over the back, through the neck to the contact (bit) so the rider can put the energy back through the horse's belly muscles to his hind legs, thus creating a "Circle of Energy."

Now imagine a two-lane road. If you have an accident in one lane (a blockage in the connection described above), you do not want to immediately increase the speed limit (add more energy), as many riders often do. If, say, the accident is on the bridge (the horse's loins), you need to *clear the accident* first—by creating more suppleness—*before* adding more energy. The difficulty as a rider is being good enough to feel where the accident is, in other words, where the horse has lost the connection, "throughness," or suppleness. This is where experience comes into play!

Q Who should decide how much contact there should be? The horse or the rider?

A The rider must be in charge of the contact. If she is always following the horse, the horse will take charge. The horse must be rewarded for the right response, so when I say the rider must be in control, it does not mean that she should force the horse into a contact or frame. The horse must learn to trust but also respect the hands, and *all* the aids.

AHA! Moment

My "Aha!" moment came when I realized what I was seeing was not what I was supposed to feel: meaning that a nice frame in front of me doesn't always equal the horse moving evenly in balance from behind. Letting go of the image of a frame and embracing the feeling of equal pushing from behind came from watching my horses while long-lining. Allowing "push" from behind will eventually lead the front end to settle into the horse's natural frame. I had been riding the frame instead of creating the energy and swing from behind.

Janet says: The frame is just a single moment, not the moving picture!

Q It took forever to figure out that contact needs to come to my hands rather than me chasing the contact around with my hands. Seems so simple now, but I wish someone had explained it to me eons ago. Can you elaborate why this took me so long?

A Frequently, a rider cannot get the correct feel with the reins because she has a fault in her seat or upper body position. Correct contact starts with a supple and secure seat and good core strength. Each horse is an individual, as well, and some horses like less contact, while others sometimes need a bit more contact momentarily to help balance all that power from the hind legs. "Feelings" are hard to explain and even harder to teach!

Your riding position is so important for this reason. The horse must learn to come to you; you cannot follow him around trying to find him. An insecure horse really needs a rider with a solid position, so when he gets out of balance, he knows exactly where the rider is and learns to allow the rider to help him rebalance. Too many riders think at the beginning with a green horse, that he needs to find the right frame right away. This is not true. The rider needs to help the horse find a frame in which he is comfortable 90 percent of the time.

It's the same thing with the tempo of the trot. Once you have submission 90 percent of the time, you are ready to change things. Trying to make changes all the time just confuses the horse.

Q Would it help to have my student ride my well-trained horse in order to get the correct feel with the reins? I was thinking of offering her a lesson on him.

A I totally agree, and with a green horse and a green rider, dressage is going to take a long time. A well-trained schoolmaster that was ridden with suppleness and a correct contact will do more for a student's riding in one lesson than 100 lessons on her green or lower-level mount. Once the rider has learned the wrong feel, it is difficult to correct it. Habits are hard to break, so it is important to think about creating the best habits in your riding right from the beginning. The idea of a rider and horse "learning" together only slows the process down and frustrates everyone.

Q I'm wondering about pushing the horse forward into contact rather than taking up the contact with the hands. Can you explain the "feel" of a forward-thinking hand? It's not always taught well to lower-level dressage "newbies."

A Yes, the rider must "push" the horse toward the bit, but the rider is also in charge of the contact. Too many riders take whatever contact the horse desires, not what the rider needs. As I've stated, 2 to 5 pounds in each rein is about right: this will be elastic and can change a bit. I see too many riders allowing the horse to just *hang* in the contact and not really *reach* into it. I mentioned the old German saying about how the horse must first learn to *lean on* the bit (see p. 79)— put another way, saying that the horse must

be "heavy" before he can be light, is very true. The lightness comes from the way he is carrying the hind legs and the elevation of his shoulders. A one-pound contact will not be sufficient to ensure your horse is really correct.

Q A really hard concept is the idea of using both reins— I see so many who believe it all should be done with the outside rein and inside leg, which results in twisted faces and crooked horses! Also, how should I push the horse forward into the contact without getting a "leaning" horse? I seem to just get more forward with a heavy, leaning horse rather than a connected, "through" horse working from his haunches.

A It is important to remember that horses need to be ridden with diagonal aids. So, for example, when the inside leg is the active leg, the outside rein and leg should be the supporting aids, with the inside rein the suppling rein. When you need to increase your bending aids, your outside leg behind the girth works with a little more active inside rein. The only time the active hand and leg are on the same side of the horse is the aid for the flying change when you close one door and open the other in the air.

As far as having energy ruin your horse's balance and thus having him lean too much in your hand, there could be several culprits. First, check your *suppleness*. Are the back and neck muscles really supple and conducting the energy in the correct way, or is there perhaps, some tension (a roadblock) there? If all is good, then look at the *straightness*. A horse with his haunches falling in and his shoulders falling out will lean on you for support, for sure. Make sure you use your shoulder-fore all the time to keep him straight. Then, with all systems go, work on transitions and be sure, when he responds correctly, to reward him with your voice, or a little pat and a softening of the contact for a moment.

....

Q Can you give some tips on working a defensive, sensitive horse into a nice frame, when he wants to evade the bit. (He will back up when he's frustrated.)

A A very sensitive horse will dislike being held in a "box" for too long. With this type, I suggest a lot of variety: change the frame a lot, throw in a lot of stretch circles or free walks to allow the brain to settle and body to relax. Doing a lot of half-halts might actually make him tenser, so think about using the movements that help collect (slow down) the horse to help with this goal: some shoulder-in, a few 10-meter circles, and leg-yielding on the circle with bend to improve the suppleness and connection to the outside rein. Do lots of logical transitions,

as well, to help the horse learn to pay attention to you.

It is a fine line between doing too much, which creates more tension, and doing nothing and boring the horse to death, which then allows him to take over! How? If the rider is not asking the horse to react to her aids, the horse will test her, and then she will have to react to the horse.

....

Q How much weight should we have in our hands for a correct contact?

A When Steffen Peters and I do our symposiums together, we like to say you should have 2 to 5 pounds in your hands. This, of course, is changeable—for example, it's not like you have 5 pounds in both reins all the time. Interestingly, Hillary Clayton—veterinarian, researcher, and author—has also done a study with weight measurements on the reins, and she found 6 pounds was the maximum the horse liked, and it was when the shoulders were coming down in the canter.

Each horse will be quite different, too. I had a Trakehner that liked about 2 or 3 pounds all the time; then I had a Holsteiner that liked 4 to 5 pounds most of the time. The key is whether this contact is elastic and supple. A very light contact can be wrong when it is "dead" and hanging. A very heavy contact can be wrong for the same reason. Dressage riders often misuse the term *lightness* by thinking that it refers to the weight in the reins. They think that if the horse has no contact then they must have lightness. This is not true. A horse with no contact

---

AHA! Moment

....

My "Aha!" moment was many years ago. I was riding a continuous 10-meter circle, when the horse wrapped himself around my inner leg, gave me a place to sit on my inner seat bone, and softened by himself on the inside rein, connecting to the outside rein. Glorious!

Janet says: HOORAY!

can be very heavy in the shoulders. So lightness must refer to the lightness of the horse's shoulders and their mobility.

Q **It is amazing how simple and how hard contact is. I think riding a horse that is good in the contact helps a rider with a horse that may struggle, and for me, riding with a trainer who can see every time I fail to push my horse into the contact and calls me on it, even when it was unconscious, helped a lot to get the idea! How often do I need to take lessons? Should I buy a schoolmaster to help me learn the correct reactions?**

A You are right in that riding a horse that is totally correct in his reaction to the aids is the most beneficial thing a rider can do. This will help the rider get the correct "feel," then be able to transfer this to her own horse. Also, having a good trainer with a lot of experience through the FEI levels is more helpful than riding with someone who has never trained a horse to that level.

Riders seeking lessons need to make a distinction between what prospective trainers really are: Did they train horses up through the levels, working step by step with each movement and training issue? Or, did they only buy "made" horses, already trained, and then rode and competed at that level? To me, there is a huge difference between the two. The trainer who goes step by step through the process will have so much more knowledge about how to deal with evasions and work through problems than the one who was only the rider on a horse that already knew his stuff. Riding the movements

and knowing the correct aids is one thing, but knowing the process is another altogether. Take as many lessons as you can afford, but also give yourself time on your own to practice!

Q **Supple elbows! Why are these so tricky to maintain?**

A Elbows can be difficult depending on the length of your arms. I have short arms, and if my elbows are on my hips, then my hands are in my lap. I had to learn to keep my hands out in front of me, with less bending in the elbow, to get the right feeling on the reins. I think too many riders "lock" their elbows to their hips, which then limits the give and take they can have through their arms.

Q **How can I achieve the best, most constant connection?**

A You need to think of an elastic rubber band, one that expands and follows the horse's topline when necessary—such as in the walk when the topline moves the most—and a little in the canter. You should be able to "firm up" the rubber band a bit as you push the horse's hind legs more under the body and over a supple back into your hand. This firm feeling is only momentary, however. If you don't return to the *supple* rubber band you will be pulling and the horse will have a short neck, among other problems that can occur. Learning "timing"—when to hold, when to let go and soften, and when to use one rein a tad to loosen the horse—is a technique and a "feel" that takes time to learn.

Q **Contact changes as you reach the higher levels: it needs to be there but self-carriage requires less contact. Is this a correct understanding?**

A Self-carriage really addresses the horse's balance and the elevation and mobility of the shoulders. It doesn't mean the horse must have *less* contact. Less contact may happen of course, but the key is to maintain a supple and elastic contact with the horse. A rein that is looping all the time is not really correct, either. Horses are individuals, and as I've mentioned, some types and breeds like a bit less contact, while other very powerful and elastic movers will require a bit more.

Q **Please talk about horses that are held together in a false frame.**

A I think that when you say "false frame" you are really talking about a "headset." Revisit page 9 where I talked about this as being a horse that is being ridden from front to back. I think we all need to keep in mind that good riding should consider the entire horse. Yes, the hind legs need to be active and working, but the bridge (back) that carries the energy must be supple and loose, also. When the horse is tense in the back, there is often tension in the contact as well. His back muscles are not correctly carrying the energy through his body to the bit. Problems with contact very rarely start in the mouth; they usually come from behind the

saddle. You need to be a detective to discover where the horse is working incorrectly.

Q **How much weight should I have in my reins to become a correct rider?**

A *Contact* is very misunderstood. Often, riders confuse *lightness* with the contact. In dressage, the term *lightness* refers to the balance of the horse, *not* how much weight there is in the reins. I have ridden many types and breeds of horses, and some like to have more contact and some less, but a big powerful horse at times will be very light in the shoulders and very mobile, but will have, let's say, 4 pounds weight in each rein. On the other hand, a Trakehner type or Arabian will also be very light in the shoulders and very mobile, but only have 2 pounds in each rein.

Q **I'm currently struggling with contact. I've had people who have suggested forcing contact, and other people who say contact comes naturally with balance and impulsion. I prefer to think it comes with balance and impulsion. What is right?**

A It is a little of both thoughts, really. The rider is responsible for the contact, not the horse. Some horses will just lean on you given their own way, and others will avoid the contact altogether. You need to find a contact that the horse will accept, and that you can maintain in an elastic way. Sometimes, this contact will "look" wrong, in that the horse might be too short in the neck, or perhaps the horse might be a bit too strung out. I am a firm believer that you need to work with the 90 percent rule: once you have the horse in the same contact 90 percent of the time, you can then start to adjust it. This adjustability is what comes with balance and impulsion.

Q Having started as a Western rider—loose rein, on a neck-reined mare—I feel that my contact needs improvement. I took a dressage clinic on a Friesian with a German instructor and he said my contact was "tentative." Can you advise?

A I rode Western as well, so it does take a bit of time to understand how the contact in dressage is more than just the weight of the reins. You will find as you learn that horses will differ in how much contact they will like. Just remember the idea of having a *rubber band* or *elastic feel* with the horse's mouth; your contact is *not* there to provide a fifth leg!

Q I am so tired of hearing about "frame." I think few trainers seem to truly teach about riding a horse into contact, riding a horse's body uphill, riding the horse's body "round." Instead, people focus on the head and neck. What is the answer?

A As mentioned above, we need to see the whole horse and then notice the small details. For example, maybe the horse with the perfect looking frame is not "through" his back. Or, perhaps the horse that sometimes comes behind the vertical is actually working well through his body, and only loses his balance occasionally. With a living, breathing animal in motion, there is so much to consider.

AHA! Moment

My "Aha!" moment was feeling like my horse was stiff on the right rein and unwilling to bend right, then realizing it is because he was subtly falling out the left shoulder. So I fixed the left shoulder and the right side became suppler.

Janet says: As a horse gets more "finished," he'll stop using the swinging croup against us; then even start to move his rib cage. Watch out for those pesky shoulders, however!

CHAPTER EIGHT

Impulsion
(SCHWUNG)

I hope the old adage of, "Forward!" as being the most important part of dressage is over! I remember having trainers chase me around with a longe whip. This maybe worked well for the old-style Warmbloods, but it was *not* helpful with the Arabians and Thoroughbreds I rode!

ENERGY WITH ELASTICITY

What really is *impulsion*? For me, the word is about *energy with elasticity*. The horse is like a fine-tuned Ferrari—lots of horsepower willing to go forward but waiting for the rider's aids. *Speed*, as in a racehorse, is not impulsion. *Forward* is a direction. Remember, we want dressage horses not racehorses. We must appreciate the horse's willingness to go forward, but speed can be used against us if we are not careful. The German term, *Schwung*, very clearly indicates this "swing" in the gaits.

Speed can cause the horse to run downhill onto his shoulders. Speed can create faster, shorter strides, rather than elastic, longer ones. Speed can cause the horse to lean on the bit and shorten the neck and curl up. Speed is not a good thing in dressage! Remember, *submission before impulsion*. Suppleness, suppleness, and more suppleness.

There are many types of horses. When Warmbloods first came into the United States, we loved the powerful trots, and especially admired the ones that hovered with lots of suspension and elasticity. Why? Well, truthfully, our Arabians and Thoroughbreds did not have this type of elasticity. But over the years, trainers wanting to get to Grand Prix realized that those slow Warmblood hind legs were not helpful in the piaffe or canter pirouettes. Even the one-tempi changes suffered. Passage was excellent, but other Grand Prix movements were difficult to train.

GO LIKE THE WIND!

True impulsion should have elasticity as well as mobility of the shoulders, balance, and a degree of harmony. There is a story that drove this point home to me.

• STORY FROM THE ROAD •

TAKING FLIGHT

I fly over a 100,000 miles a year, and have over 2 million frequent flyer miles on United Airlines. I also have about 750,000 miles on Delta Airlines. So, I am often asked if I am ever afraid of flying...I can admit to it once, and I remember it well!

I went to Jackson Hole, Wyoming, for many years to teach. I had started clinics in the area in Idaho Falls at Rick and Shannon Reed's arena behind their home. I have so many wonderful memories from those clinics, and that is where I first met Joan Darnell. Her now beautiful and grownup daughter Claire, was still in diapers.

Robin and Bill Weiss built the Spring Creek Equestrian Center in Jackson Hole. Since the Reeds did not have an indoor, we moved the clinics to a year-round event facility. One of my former working students Kris Montgomery went to work for the Weiss's, so it was a great group of people and we had a lot of fun.

However, this did cause a change in my flights. I was flying Delta then in a large Boeing to Idaho Falls. However, a very small Brasilia aircraft flew into Jackson Hole. And remember, clinics were now year-round, and let me tell you, it can snow in Jackson Hole!

Bad weather moved in, but we finished the clinic. The arena was heated, as was the entire barn, so we did not suffer at all. I went to the airport and found out that they had cancelled most of the flights from Salt Lake City to Jackson. Robin asked their pilot to fly me down and he refused, saying the reports of turbulence were disturbing. Hmmm. Yes, I should have just gone back to the Weiss's home and spent another night and had another great dinner. But I am stubborn and all of my training horses and students were waiting for me on Monday, and I sort of felt like the mail—neither snow nor turbulence was going to stop me.

Finally a plane landed. As we went up the steps the flight attendant handed me a large bag. I asked what it was for. She said, "The small bags are not working well." Again, I should have turned around and marched down those little stairs. But not me! I must say very few people joined me on this flight, which was probably a good thing—if someone throws up, it is all over for me.

So, we took off and I was thinking it would only be bad on the climb out. Wrong. The good news was that it was only a 45-minute flight. Bad news was that we were flying sideways and up and down the entire time. I was green when I deplaned. The attendant said she had to fly back up there. I told her I would quit if it were me.

Now if I am ever afraid, I just remember the worst flight I was ever on—that one! Then I am all good.

Many years ago, I had two top horses, one a sensitive Swedish Warmblood and one a not-as-sensitive Holsteiner. They were two different personalities and had to be trained with two different approaches. The coaches I worked with when they were younger (Kay Meredith and Robert Dover) were great with both types of horses. They could relax a tense horse and wake up a dull one.

When the United States was looking for a new dressage coach, several candidates came through the country giving clinics. I had them all in Colorado, and one was a disaster. I had, of course, asked this person what breakfast choices needed to be available at my house. When the first morning arrived, I was informed that I did not have the right cereal. I was sent to the store to correct my error.

Then during the lessons, it was all about speed: Go, Go, Go, and Go More with both horses. The Holsteiner merely looked at the longe whip and said, "Ho hum, okey dokey, no problem." The Swedish horse's eyeballs popped out of the sides of his head. This clinician was very pleased with the Swedish horse, telling everyone how wonderful the trot was during the lesson. It did not seem to matter to him that I could not stop or turn, or that I had 50 pounds in each rein.

I am always polite to a person teaching me. I try to do what is asked. However, in this case, I did not bring this horse back the next day; rather, I gave that session to someone else. I really prefer to work with someone who knows how to deal with many different types and personalities of horses, instead of someone who only has one system and demands that every horse fit into that system. The final straw was when this coach tried to ask for more pay than we had agreed. Needless to say, there was no return clinic booked at my barn!

The point of this story is that *speed is not impulsion*. True impulsion needs harmony and the rider should have the ability to softly influence that impulsion, not just hang on for dear life. A horse with true impulsion will be able to make good transitions, to turn, and be balanced enough not to lean on the rider's hands for support. A horse with only speed needs to lean on the rider's hands, and it takes too much strength to stop and turn him.

"SLOWER" VS. "QUICKER" HIND LEG

Eventually in dressage, the "quicker" hind leg became a bit more popular. Also, we came to realize that the canter was very important. Many of the modern dressage horses are very quick and active behind, but the elasticity of their trot might suffer a bit at first. However, with correct training and working the horse correctly through the topline, the elasticity can develop.

Which kind of trot do I now recommend for you? If you want to do well up through Second or Third Level, either will do, and perhaps the more elastic horse with a natural, slower trot tempo will score even higher at the lower levels. After that, however, the "slower" hind leg will give you some training issues.

The most important part of the message to remember, however, is that without *suppleness* and a correct *contact*, impulsion will never really happen. The Training Pyramid must be followed in order for the natural balance and natural gaits of the horse to be improved.

~ PROBLEMS ~
and Solutions

Q What is "in front of the leg"? I thought I had "got it," but when my horse really became in front of the leg, I realized I had been wrong for years!

A It would be too easy if *in front of the leg* just meant kicking the horse a lot and running around faster and faster! The real meaning is making sure the horse has a quick reaction to a light aid. The rider is responsible for this, and must be sure she doesn't keep using a stronger and stronger leg for less and less of a reaction. The horse truly in front of the leg will want to show a willingness to go, but also be supple through his topline so that his muscles can carry the "electricity" (energy) from the hind legs, up over the back, through the neck, to the mouth, then return through the muscles of the belly. As we've discussed, this is called the Circle of Energy, if you will (see also p. 68).

Q How do I know if I have impulsion in my riding?

A Impulsion is a word that means *suspension* and *elasticity* as well as energy to move the horse forward and up off the ground. A racehorse is forward but has speed: there is little suspension in his gait because that suspension would slow the horse down. Speed is not impulsion. It is only a "direction," just like the word "forward." Engagement is stored energy. The hind leg that is on the ground, with bending joints just like a coiled spring, is an *engaged* hind leg. Impulsion is the release of that spring, pushing the horse up off, then over, the ground. So if you can ride in a way that you don't have to drive your

horse every stride, and he takes care of this himself for a few strides, you are on the right track. Then, he should also be able to show some transitions between the paces, such as working trot to trot lengthening, back to working trot.

Q What is the difference between speed, forward, and real impulsion?

A You are talking about an interesting concept. Let's think of energy or electricity. Engagement is like stored energy. The hind leg stays on the ground and the joints bend and compress like a spring. Then, when the electricity or energy is released from the hind leg, the spring will jump up in the air first. This is *impulsion*—the idea is that the energy goes *off* the ground before it goes *over* the ground. *Speed* or simply a direction to go *forward* may cover ground, but this energy will be very earthbound.

Q Hard concepts are *forward* and *in front of your leg* without chasing the horse—instead, getting the correct activity from behind. It seems when we get this concept contact becomes easier. When I am struggling with *forward*, I try to force the roundness and end up pulling instead of pushing to the contact. Help.

A When a rider runs the horse off his feet, the hind legs will lose their ability to bend their joints, and will fall way out behind the tail. This type of energy is totally wrong for dressage. Hind legs need to bend in the joints and stay in front of the tail to support the horse.

Sometimes, developing this ability and strength means the trot gets a bit "boring," but when you add too much power before the horse is strong enough to support himself, he can get tense in the back and lose all suspension. Try using your transitions within a shoulder-in to help you get the inside hind leg more under the horse's body, and by displacing the shoulders a bit more, you should be able to balance the horse more uphill in the shoulders, which should also help lighten the contact.

Make sure that when you add energy or electricity from the hind legs, it is not like a deep-sea fishing expedition. If you are

deep-sea fishing and you hook a large fish, and it takes the hook (the bit) and then dives to the bottom of the ocean, you will be pulled out of your chair. (You see why they belt you into it!) Impulsion must first have submission and suppleness and a correct connection—or you won't be able to balance and control the energy. Think instead of fly fishing (see p. 82).

Q **Why does impulsion come after suppleness in the Training Pyramid?**

A The answer is simple, really. Energy must travel through supple muscles and have a connection from the hind legs to the contact. If your horse does not have this supple connection, the energy from the hind legs does not create true impulsion. You will have speed, and the strides will be shorter and quicker rather than springy and more ground-covering.

Q **Why do instructors keep saying more leg, more forward? Forward isn't about speed, correct?**

A Yes, *forward* is only a direction. Impulsion is about elasticity and suppleness. More leg is never the answer either, as that only makes the horse harder to ride. The answer is a quicker, correct response to the leg and seat. The energy recirculating is about the suppleness, and working the topline muscles in the correct way so that we are able to send the energy from the hind legs to the bit and back again through the belly muscles.

AHA! Moment

Mine was realizing that all that suppleness we think we have at the lower levels is ever so more important at FEI. Once I realized how much more I needed during all the movements and spent time accomplishing this, my scores went up several percentage points.

Janet says: I like to say that if your instructor tells you it gets easier at the FEI Levels, he is not telling you the truth. It gets different, but the suppleness requirement actually increases, the angles in the half-passes become more oblique, and the horse is required to show the maximum elasticity of the strides and the topline. Going from extensions to either piaffe or canter pirouettes are an example of this elasticity.

However, the idea about *being forward in the halt* is important. The rider should feel at all times that the energy or electricity running through the horse's muscles could become an extension, a pirouette, or a halt. The amount of rpms (energy) should be the same at all times. The rider shouldn't feel that she must create more energy because an extension is coming up—the energy should already be present in the collection.

A trainer should not ask a rider to be stronger with the leg—that just makes the horse duller to it! The horse should be quick off the *go* aids, then the rider should reward the horse so he knows he did the right thing.

Q Why does dressage put such a high premium on "bouncy" types of horses?

A If you think about the movements that require a lot of suspension, such as the passage and the medium trot, you will start to understand why elasticity is so important. But equally important is how the horse uses his hind legs. Many horses are very elastic, but with very slow and straight hind legs. This type of horse does well at the lower levels. Once collection is required, however, those hind legs need to bend and articulate. Why? There are movements in dressage that require a quick tempo, too, such as piaffe and canter pirouettes.

Q Why is the word "engagement" in the Collective Marks for Training and First Level under impulsion? I thought these levels did not require engagement.

A These levels don't require engagement in the sense that the horse should be uphill. Instead, they require the horse to be in a "level" balance. The USEF Dressage Committee discussed this at great length. The decision was based on the concept that in dressage, the horse should be in the *correct balance for the level*. So in that sense, a Training Level horse should have enough engagement or balance to stay in a "level" balance and not be downhill and falling on the shoulders.

Q If I have a horse with terrible lengthenings, where will I be marked down in the test?

A You will receive a lower mark in the movement score, and your impulsion score will also be lowered. The impulsion score at First Level and above will include how well you and your horse are able to perform the lengthenings.

CHAPTER NINE

Straightness
(GERADERICHTUNG)

Straightness is another confusing piece of the Training Pyramid. And, unfortunately, if you don't understand it, your horse will never reach the top of the Pyramid, which is *collection*. When you have managed to create a supple topline and elastic contact and have harnessed the power of the hind legs for impulsion, you will have to now address straightness.

LINE OF TRAVEL

With straightness, think of "line of travel" rather than thinking of the horse as having to look like the numeral "1," or a lower-case "l." This would be a stiff horse! There are only two movements in dressage where the front legs or forehand are on the line of travel: travers (haunches-in) and half-pass. In both, the forehand is placed on the line of travel and the haunches are displaced. In travers, the forehand moves down the track, and in half-pass, the forehand moves along a diagonal line. In every other movement, the hind legs are placed on the line of travel and the forehand is displaced in front of the hind leg you want to engage.

So when you are riding on a straight line, such as the centerline or the long side, you want to think of riding a shoulder-fore to make the horse straight. Or, perhaps a slight bit of renvers (haunches-out), which will connect the horse from the inside leg to the outside rein, as well. Whichever method you use to straighten your horse will depend on his level of training.

Stiff vs. Supple Side

Another consideration is to decide which is the horse's stiff side or supple side. Let's use for our example a horse that is stiff on the left side. This means he is left-side-long and right-side-short. Another way to express this is that the horse likes to bend right (his hollow side) and doesn't like to bend left (his stiff side). This horse is like a person who is right-handed. The right side is more coordinated but the left side is the stronger side.

Going to the right, this horse will love to bend right. However, he will usually fall out on the left outside shoulder, because doing this will help his weaker right hind leg. So riding this horse in a right shoulder-fore to straighten him won't really work. Using a slight renvers right, will work the right hind and stop the horse from falling out over the left shoulder.

Going to the left, this horse will resist bending left so the shoulder-fore or the slight renvers will be helpful. Both movements will ask the horse to move off the inside leg and step toward the outside rein. Using the renvers on the straight line will be very helpful. Remember as the training progresses, the rider's job is to ask the horse to shorten his left side and, therefore, stretch his right side, which this horse does not find comfortable.

When the horse is strong enough to do piaffe, passage, or the one-tempi changes, you will have the ability to ride the horse like a numeral "1," because both of his hind legs are carrying the weight equally. Rein-back is the one movement in the lower levels where you also want the horse straight like a "1." Although I find that halting the horse in a little shoulder-fore prior to the rein-back helps him to rein-back without pushing the haunches off the rail.

Control of the line of travel allows you to control the engagement. The horse, not being fond of this idea, will try to take the straightness away from you: his haunches will swing in or out, or perhaps the shoulders will fall in or out. Sometimes, as the haunches fall in, the outside shoulder also falls out.

IT'S ABOUT MOBILITY

Why is straightness so important? In dressage, we want to have the horse mobile. Think of the canter zigzags, for instance. Quickly changing direction and staying in an uphill balance requires a lot of strength as well as mobility. The horse likes stability. In other words, he wants to spread his legs and have the balance a bit to the shoulders. When the horse is stable (as in Training or First Level), you won't have the ability to put the horse uphill, nor will you be able to do the "cool moves" of the upper levels!

So, straightness is a must in order to create mobility.

STRAIGHT ON THE LINE OF TRAVEL

In A we see a horse "straight" on a curved line, in other words, following the line of travel.

In B the horse is not straight, rather the hindquarters have moved in and the outside shoulder has moved out.

Drawing C shows a horse correct in shoulder-fore, or straight on the line of travel.

In D the horse is not straight as he is falling on the outside shoulder.

Drawing E depicts a horse in correct shoulder-in.

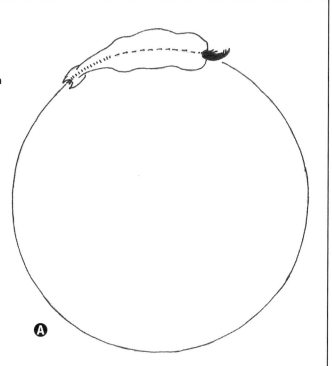

A

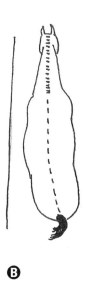

B

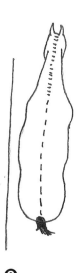

C

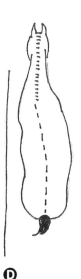

D

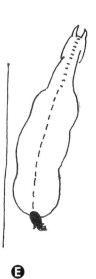

E

TWIST AND SHOUT

For years, I was always concerned about the horse's haunches falling in. This seemed to be a major issue with all the horses I trained. Along with the haunches falling in, of course, was the issue of the outside shoulder falling out. Finally, one horse taught me the value of the outside leg behind the girth in a rather spectacular way.

Electus was an unbroken three-year-old Swedish stallion when I bought him. He was a bright chestnut, with four white socks and a blaze. He was a Furioso II son, and eventually, due to his dislike for collection, was sold as a hunter, where he excelled.

The dressage arena at my barn was a permanent arena, made of welded metal, and the footing a mix of sand and rubber. In other words, noiseless. Electus and I rode in this arena in preparation for our first show. Aspen Dressage held a marvelous show at Sandy Smith's farm in Carbondale, Colorado. My group loved to go up there and show; even the long drive over the mountain passes did not dampen our enthusiasm.

I was riding in my first test of the show, a Training Level test. Electus was four years old. In the first turn at C, his haunches fell out. This was only because of tension in his back, as he was a bit nervous about his first time in the arena. Sandy had the newest type of arena, what we call the "California arena" with plastic holders and PVC pipe rails. She also had coarse sand footing. Well, as the haunches fell out, a hoof full of sand hit the corner boxes and the PVC pipe. It made a loud noise and Electus was sure he was being chased by something evil. He bolted across the arena only to splash sand again on the other side. He then spun and ran backward, splashing more sand as he went. It was a miracle I got him stopped in the middle near the centerline. I quickly dismounted and excused myself from the ring—on foot!

I am sure we provided the judge with her morning entertainment. Needless to say that afternoon we spent time throwing sand at things that made noise and giving Electus sugar. I also was careful about my outside leg behind the girth in the next test, and yes, he was a star and ended up winning his class the second time out!

~ PROBLEMS ~
and Solutions

Q I continue to struggle with the concept of shoulder-fore. Help!

A Shoulder-fore is the best straightening aid *ever*. Think of the line of travel, in other words, where do you want your horse to go? As I've said, there are only two movements in dressage that have the forehand on the line of travel: travers and half-pass. All other movements have the hind legs on the line of travel and the shoulders slightly displaced. The shoulder-fore and the "baby" renvers (which has the same tracking as the shoulder-fore, but is counterflexed rather than slightly bending to the inside) are also great methods to help keep the horse connected from the inside leg to the outside rein. For specific instructions in how to use the shoulder-fore, please see *Dressage for the Not-So-Perfect Horse*.

Q I think one of the hardest concepts for me to grasp and feel was that of a truly aligned horse pushing equally from both hind legs. This includes truly aligned lateral work and "throughness." I don't want to show until I really understand these concepts. What can I do to make sure I am really "getting it?"

A Yes, it takes an educated rider with a lot of miles to develop that feel of equal engagement. I think that too many riders, and trainers too, tend to accept little deviations of straightness or a reaction to an aid that is a bit dull. When this happens, the horse that is more than happy to just be out in the field eating grass takes advantage of the rider. The concept of having a horse that is equally supple in both directions is a goal I often hear. However, often these riders are very crooked themselves and only seem to want to work on the horse.

Q I need help with achieving straightness!

A As you can see, this is a common problem! Throughout the horse's training, it is important for the rider to pay attention to straightness. This evasion never goes away; even Grand Prix riders will struggle with this issue. Keep checking your alignment when you come off a circle onto a straight line.

AHA! Moment

My "Aha!" moment is related to the dilemma of seeing what the neck appears to be doing versus what the rest of the horse is actually doing: bending longitudinally and laterally are so interrelated. I remember a brilliant flash of lucidity from Dr. Gail Hoff-Carmona when she informed a rider, "The key to longitudinal suppleness (collection, bend, and engagement) is lateral suppleness." Of course, the art of training is how to put this together to improve the horse: easy in concept, painting the Sistine chapel in practice!

Janet says: Yes, it sounds easy when standing on the ground, harder when you are on the horse!

Remember to think about how to start and finish all of your exercises so that you keep building on the collection and balance the exercise created.

Q **I'd like some tips on helping a horse with a hind end that travels like he's on a tight rope rather than tracking straighter. Can this horse develop a better hind end, balance, and way of going?**

A Some horses are difficult to change much due to their conformation issues. A horse that "rope-walks" behind—or in front—can be helped a little bit with shoeing and some lateral-suppling exercises, like head-to-the-wall leg-yields or leg-yielding off a straight line. Using some bending, which will displace the shoulders a bit and put the inside hind leg more under the body can also be helpful.

Q **Straightness and timing! Timing of the aids! Explain these in regard to the half-halt.**

A Let's address the *timing* issue. Timing is something that usually needs to be learned. Few riders are born with a natural instinct. Those that are usually have a hard time teaching timing to someone else. The best teachers are usually people who have had to struggle with the timing issue themselves.

We have three aids. Our seat, our legs, and our hands. We need to be able to communicate with the horse using only these aids, and perhaps our voice as well, in training.

Learning about what each aid is supposed to do is important because we have a knack for using the wrong aid to fix a problem. In fact, at first, our brain seems to always tell us the wrong thing. For example: Lean forward. Pull on the reins. Always kick first. So, using our brain and really thinking through the problem is the best way to learn about timing. It is much better to do nothing than to do the wrong thing.

As regards the half-halt, see page 9 for discussion of when and how to use it.

Q **How do I make my horse straight?**

A Straightness is one of the most misunderstood concepts in dressage in the United States. As I explained earlier on, here it is a one-word element of the Training Pyramid, yet if we were to translate the German word *Geraderichtung*, it would take several sentences in English. The word really means "riding the horse along the correct line of travel." So, knowing that, except in travers and half-pass, the hind legs are always on the line of travel, you know you must slightly position the shoulders in front of the hindquarters for the horse to be truly straight. This is the idea of shoulder-fore. The horse in a slight renvers is also straight. Straightness means the horse is connected from the inside leg to the outside rein.

Naturally, the horse is like a little red wagon or an old-fashioned four-wheel roller skate (see p. 44) that is in a very stable but not a very mobile balance. This is just fine with the horse. Dressage riders, however, want the horse in an "unstable" balance and more mobile so he can do the "cool" movements. So think of your inside leg as pushing the inside leg of the horse forward and across his body. This puts his inside hind leg slightly in front of his outside hind leg. Then, with your reins, you move the shoulders slightly to the inside, or in other words, you put the outside shoulder slightly in front of the inside front leg. You now have a horse that, rather than being like the four-wheel roller skate, has his legs like an in-line roller skate. You have more mobility and less stability.

AHA! Moment

My "Aha!" moment came the day I learned the truth about straightness: riding the spine straight, not the outside of the horse, was the biggest change in how I rode any horse I got on, regardless of his age, training, breed, or discipline.

Janet says: I think this area of training is highly misunderstood. The idea is that the horse must be on the lines of travel, with the body moving along those lines. Too many riders think straightness means hanging on the outside rein, and never using the inside rein. Consequently, the horse is like an "L" and stiffer than a board; he runs around with a short neck and his hind legs out behind.

The rider needs to understand some biomechanics of how the horse uses his muscles. The shoulders and neck must be positioned slightly in front of the hind legs, and his belly must be pushed slightly out. This allows the abdominal muscles to contract and pull the inside hind leg more under the body, and step more toward the outside rein. The rider must put the horse in a shoulder-fore for this to happen.

CHAPTER TEN

Collection
(VERSAMMLUNG)

Collection is at the top of the Training Pyramid and the one element of the Pyramid we are all seeking. The horse is in an uphill balance with good lateral suppleness, connected over his back with mobile shoulders, and in excellent control over the line of travel—that is, *straightness*.

THE GOAL

Our goal as riders and trainers is to create a horse that is more comfortable to ride, one that is willing and capable at the task at hand.

Many riders will show their horse at Second Level or Fourth Level or even the FEI Levels, because their horse has learned the movements required in those levels. However, just doing a flying change doesn't a Third Level horse make! The real issue that judges see over and over again is the lack of the correct balance relative to the requirements of the Level. What does this mean?

When the horse is in the correct balance for that Level, the movements will flow from one to another, and the transitions between the paces will be clear, supple, and smooth. Without correct balance, the horse will struggle with movements, and transitions will be downhill and stiff, with the hind legs escaping out behind the horse.

Collection takes time. It involves the correct training and development of the horse's suppleness and strength. Each year, the rider should see a more beautiful and muscular physique on her horse. When you do, you are correctly gymnasticizing his muscles. The physique of the horse is often a telling indicator about the ability of the horse to perform up to the standards of a dressage test.

HOW DO YOU GET TO SELF-CARRIAGE?

Following the Training Pyramid and doing correct gymnastic work develops self-carriage. If your horse is not able to make shorter higher steps, he will not be able to extend. Remember the Pendulum of Elasticity (see p. 12). Creating a strong and elastic topline and abdominal muscles that can bring the horse's hind legs under his body, then hold them there so they can carry weight, is the key to self-carriage. A horse without a correctly muscled body will not have self-carriage.

Both Hind Legs Must Push Equally

If your horse is not equally supple laterally, the hind legs will not push or be able to carry equally. This means, for example, that when the horse is weaker on the right hind, the horse will push his weight over to the left shoulder instead of carrying weight on the right hind. So straightness is a major player!

Capturing the Shoulders

Not only do the hind legs need to be equal, but the rider must also be able to move the horse's shoulders around. Think of the half-pass zigzags. The shoulders must be in control: as the rider finishes one half-pass and straightens the horse for the flying change, he immediately goes into the new direction for the new half-pass. In the one-tempi changes, the rider must keep both shoulders up and mobile, or the hind legs will swing.

WORK WITHIN THE COMFORT ZONE

I think after all the years of riding and training, and working with so many different breeds and types of horses, that collection can be different from horse to horse.

Of course, there is the collection needed for a "10" in the Grand Prix movements, but I am not talking about the elite portion of our sport now—mainly because so few of us ever get there. So let's be realistic about life: your job as a rider and trainer is to develop the collection that is correct for your horse. Will the final product look like Totilas or Valegro? Probably not. However, dressage, if ridden and trained correctly, will make any horse more beautiful and more athletic. And that, at the end of the day, is what we should be proud of.

Riders should also realize their horse's limitations. Not every horse will get to Grand Prix; he may learn the movements, but developing the correct balance and collection can be difficult. There are mental considerations to take into account. My Swedish stallion

Electus was very athletic and had the talent physically for Grand Prix, but mentally he was uncomfortable being put into the correct "package" for Grand Prix. For me, it wasn't worth making him so unhappy. He had a wonderful and very successful life as a hunter after I retired him from dressage at the Small Tour level.

Other horses may not be able to develop the correct balance due to conformational difficulties. A very "downhill" horse, one with short front legs, will always look a bit downhill. A horse with hind legs that do not articulate the joints will have trouble "sitting" and carrying the weight.

My plea to all of you is to have a wonderful and happy partnership with your horse, and not to push him beyond his comfort level. I have no problem with those who choose to stay at home, training and learning the movements. But it is unfair to you, the horse, and the judge to present him at a level where he will struggle to perform.

~ PROBLEMS ~
and Solutions

Q **Collection is the most misunderstood concept in my opinion. So many people think it has to do with a shorter "frame" and they try to achieve collection starting at the front. What does collection really mean? Is it all about the neck?**

A Collection is about the horse's balance. Yes, the definition in the Rulebook talks about the neck being raised and arched, but this is only part of the picture. The term "collection" is also relative to the different levels. A horse at Second Level will just be developing collection, and it will come and go a bit. The Grand Prix horse will have the ultimate amount of collection. So, the word collection needs to encompass the *carrying ability* or *engagement* of the *hind legs*, as well as the *elevation* and *mobility* of the *shoulders*. The steps or strides in collection do get shorter and cover less ground, but to make up for that, they also get higher and have more activity.

....

Q **I know it is the rider who must create collection, but how?**

A Self-carriage is something that comes and goes. The rider wants it—the horse not so much. The rider's timing and ability to quickly discover where the horse is cheating is important. Remember, the horse can only be in self-carriage when these other pieces are in place: an active hind leg, a supple topline to carry the energy to the contact, an elastic and even contact with the bit, and straightness.

....

Q **What's the difference between collection at Second Level versus Fourth Level? Also between Prix St. Georges and Grand Prix? It's all relative and hard to know what you can expect as you go along, and how much to ask for—and when it's too much.**

A Collection changes as the horse matures in his mind, suppleness, and body. A Grand Prix horse has more muscling than a First Level horse—if he has been correctly trained. At Training and First Level, the hind legs are merely pushing the horse over the ground. At Second Level, they begin to start to carry weight, but this will come and go. At Third and Fourth Level, the horse should show more ability to carry, and there is the addition

---

AHA! Moment

....

My "Aha!" moment was when I realized lateral work is a means to an end, not the end itself. That simple realization made a whole lot of things click into place for me. Again, I wish someone had just said that to me!

Janet says: Each lateral movement is like a tool in your toolbox. Training your horse is like building a house. You need to start with the basement, then the foundation. No one can build a house from the top down. So, your turn-on-the-forehand is like your plain old screwdriver, and the leg-yield is a hammer. Finally, you have a few power tools, like the half-pass.

of the extensions that require more strength and ground coverage. At Fourth, exercises like the working pirouettes are introduced to show the horse can take more weight on the inside hind leg.

There is always a discussion at Prix St. Georges about how much collection is needed. If you have a very uphill and elastic horse by nature, he can do the whole test without much additional strengthening—except maybe the canter pirouettes. Some judges and trainers think this is okay; I personally do not, as it will be very difficult for the horse to move to the Intermediare I test and above without the correct muscling and gymnasticizing of the body. Not developing the topline correctly at this point also puts the horse in a much more precarious position for injury.

Q **I try to ride my mare toward collection each day, but many days something gets in my way. How do I figure it out?**

A Riding dressage is a bit like being a detective each day. The rider must test the horse's reactions to the aids. It may be the same as yesterday, maybe not. Sometimes, one day will be so super and the rider is so excited about the next training session. Then, *poof*, this session is all about the horse saying "No thank you, not today." It sounds like you want to have a good logical approach to your training, and believe me, you will get a lot more done that way than by being stubborn and riding with emotion. Horses really don't stand in their stalls overnight thinking up things to do to us the next day!

Sometimes, when you had an amazing day yesterday, your horse might be a bit sore, and won't want to work as hard. This might be a good day for a trail ride, or some simple stretching work and transitions.

Go through the Training Pyramid each day like a pilot does with his check list before takeoff. How is the rhythm? Is the horse supple and using the back? Haunches swinging out may be a clue here. How is the contact? Tilting or an open mouth or pulling would be a clue here. Then check the impulsion. Is he quick and light off your leg aid? Wherever there is a problem. STOP! Fix that problem before moving further up the Pyramid.

Q **When the horse's head is "on the vertical" but there is a lack of propulsion from behind, this is a "false frame," correct? And, is the horse's nose "in front of the vertical" in a Second Level test an example of a not-level-appropriate frame?**

A Judging (and riding) would be so easy if we could only look at the horse's head and say if it is good or not. But, we must all learn to look at the *whole picture* and then notice the small details. I have not heard the term "false frame" but assume you mean a "headset" (see p. 9).

The answer to your second question is: No, the horse's nose slightly in front of the vertical with the poll the highest point is desirable at *all* the levels. And remember, we need to look at the entire horse—not just a still picture or a movement in time but rather a *moving* picture that gives all the information we need to make these kind of judgments.

Q **If I ride the hind legs with enough energy will the shoulders elevate?**

A I rode for years thinking if I just got the hind legs going fast enough the shoulders would rise like a miracle. Didn't happen. Too easy I guess! Making sure that the shoulders are mobile and light is an important part of straightness, and without the ability to control the line of travel, collection won't happen.

CHAPTER ELEVEN

Dressage Movements

As a dressage judge, I see many people riding in the show ring who don't understand the basic concept of the movement they are trying to perform. I know that sometimes the horse can be difficult and evasive. For example, turn-on-the-haunches: when the rider shows the turns in both directions counterbent, I know she did not read the definition of the movement in the USEF Rulebook. The Rulebook is a great source of free information—so please take the time and read about each movement you are schooling or performing at a show.

A PURPOSE

The movements in dressage all have a purpose. They are there to help improve the horse's suppleness, his balance, and also his reaction to your aids.

I find that the movements can also help you discover where your horse needs a bit more work. I am a firm believer that if the movement is not going well, just continuing to practice it, with the same mistakes over and over again, is detrimental to the horse's training.

If you have a problem in a movement, you the rider, being the smarter of the two in the partnership, needs to figure out which aid is not working for you. Remember to break down each of the movements and stay true to the Training Pyramid! (There is a lot of detailed information in my book *Dressage for the Not-So-Perfect Horse* about the aids for each movement and how to discover the most basic cause for the resistance you may be having.)

Remember, if the Training Pyramid is correct and your basics are correct, the movement will take care of itself!

MOVEMENTS AND WHY YOU DO THEM

These movements stretch the horse, either longitudinally or laterally:

- Leg-yield
- Shoulder-in
- Travers and renvers
- Half-pass
- Stretch circle (see p. 13)

These movements improve the horse's balance (collecting movements), as well as his reaction to your aids:

- Transitions
- Shoulder-in
- Travers and renvers
- Half-pass

These movements test the horse's adjustability:

- Lengthenings, mediums, and extensions
- Transitions between the paces

These movements test the horse's "sitting" ability (engagement):

- Piaffe
- Canter pirouettes

These movements test the mobility of the shoulders:

- Walk and canter pirouettes
- Turn-on-the-haunches
- Zigzags

A NEW FREESTYLE MOVEMENT

I always thought ice-skating had it right. When you invented a movement, that movement was named after you. Remember the "Hamill Camel" named after Dorothy Hamill? I invented a new movement too, but was given no credit for it because it was not in Freestyle but rather in a regular test.

I have named the movement, "Zigzag at canter with no change of lead." The judge recognized the difficulty as well, and even mentioned it in his comment. The comment read, "High degree of difficulty, but should be ridden in Freestyle, not a normal test."

Here is my story: I cantered perfectly down centerline, ready for the 4-8-8-4. My lovely Trakehner stallion, Maroon, was a bit too smart for his own good and was always clever at invention. I was busy counting and he was busy ignoring my aids. (Must have been that pretty little filly in Ring 2.) Well, the counting was perfect, as was the bend and the geometry. It was amazing, looking back, how much bend he could have while on the wrong lead and going the wrong direction. Sigh. I think it was all of those suppling exercises I did at counter-canter, bending him the wrong direction and pushing him in a leg-yield sideways to improve the quality of the canter.

~ PROBLEMS ~
and Solutions

Q How much contact should you keep or release as you perform the "stretch circle"?

A You should have the same contact as you do when your horse is on a shorter rein. As I've said before, you can't just throw the reins away. Keep using your bending or inside rein to keep him laterally supple and then slowly lengthen the outside rein as he seeks the contact. Think of being able to half-halt with a longer rein and you will get the idea.

Q The "stretch circle" confuses me.

A The "stretchy-chewy circle," as I call it, needs to be taught to the horse gradually, not in one day. With a green or young horse, the rider must find a place in the frame where the horse will go 90 percent of the time before trying to change it. The same applies to the tempo of the trot. Once the horse has mastered the idea of stretching equally into both reins, it is time to teach him the bending aids. I find it easier to teach the stretching with his stiff side to the inside. So, if the horse doesn't like to bend left, do the circle on the left rein.

Remember, you are going to use the bending to stretch or lengthen the outside of the body, while also asking the horse to stretch and lengthen the topline a bit. Using your bending aids, be sure to push the horse's rib cage out with your inside leg, then half-halt on the outside rein. When the horse lowers his neck a bit, give a little and allow the horse to lengthen his neck a few inches.

Don't "throw the contact away." The idea is to teach him to go down a few inches more each week. Once the horse has lost the contact, you will have to shorten the reins and start again. Be sure you maintain the bend, otherwise the horse can just curl his neck and drop it, rather than honestly stretching into both reins.

Q In some dressage tests, we are told to make a transition between one letter and another, and I wonder what this means?

A In the lower-level tests, a rider is asked to make transitions between two letters so it is easier for the horse and rider to accomplish. At the FEI levels, however, a higher standard is expected and transitions need to be prompt—at the letter—and supple.

This really all relates to how well the elasticity of the horse has been developed. At First Level, the horse will not have a lot of difference between his paces. In other words, his lengthenings will be slightly more ground-covering that his working trot. In Grand Prix, however, where you have a lot of different trots, all with a different length and height of stride: the piaffe, for example, is the shortest trot; the passage is the trot that comes the most off the ground; and the extended trot is the most ground-covering. The Grand Prix horse should be able to shift between these trots smoothly and quickly, while the First Level horse only has two "gears": working and lengthening, and the transition will take more time at this level.

Q How much difference in bend should I have between a leg-yield and a half-pass?

A If you read the definitions in the USEF Rulebook, you will see that in leg-yield there is, in fact, no bend at all. The body of the horse is straight and there is a slight lateral flexion in the poll away from the direction of travel. In half-pass, there is a clear bend throughout the entire body of the horse, and this bend is in the direction of travel.

Q In the Equine Canada tests, the 20-meter circle is at A. I was wondering where the approach should be to be accurate (compared to 20-meter circles at E or B).

A If you are riding in a large dressage arena, you will have the same circle points in the arena. Think of a snowman that has three sections. There is a bottom, a middle, and a top. All three sections are the same size and they touch each other. Now think of three circles, exactly the same size, laid down in the 20- x 60-meter dressage arena. These concentric circles are accurate 20-meter circles and also the path that a width-of-the-arena, three-loop serpentine would take. Remember how many meters are between each letter. From the corners to the first letter is 6 meters. Then there is 12 meters between the other letters. So, if you used the I and L between the RSVP letters for your circle points, your circles at C and A would be too small, and you would be riding a 24-meter oval at B and E.

In a small dressage arena, this, of course, changes, as the length of the arena is only 40 meters. So here your 20-meter circles at A and C would touch X. The circle points for your 20-meter circles at B and E would need to be on the centerline, 10 meters on either side of X. For illustrations of these concepts, see the sidebar on page 119.

Q What do you do when a horse shuts down when doing a simple change? He stops, then I wait it out and he finally moves again. Am I doing something wrong? Do I need to be stronger? I always go back and review the walk and the canter.

A Usually, being stronger is never the answer. I like that you are going back and reviewing the walk and the canter, but it seems to me he has this habit a bit stuck in his brain now. You mention you are showing Fourth Level, so this is just a training exercise for you, not something you need to do in the test. I think, sometimes, we as riders are too stubborn, and perhaps here is a good chance to just go back to something more basic for a while, and allow the horse to think more forward.

I would avoid walk-canter transitions for now, and do a lot of canter-trot-canter transitions, even perhaps doing a little medium trot between the canter to help his brain think forward instead of stop, as he is doing right now. After a few weeks, you can move on again.

Maybe he doesn't see the need to do less than a flying change. He sounds like he has an opinion! My suggestion would be to supple him a bit to the left and even leg-yield a

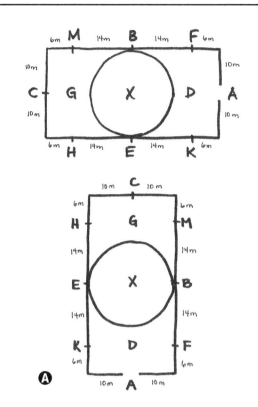

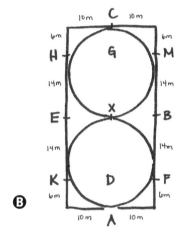

Ⓐ

Ⓑ

A GUIDE TO ACCURATE CIRCLES

Drawing A (horizontal and vertical) shows the correct placement of a 20-meter circle at B or E in a small 20- x 40-meter dressage arena.

In B (horizontal and vertical) you see the correct placement of a 20-meter circle at A or C in a small 20- x 40-meter dressage arena.

Drawing C depicts correct placement of 20-meter circles at A, C, E or B in a large 20- x 60-meter dressage arena.

In D you see the same circles as in C showing the exact location of each circle.

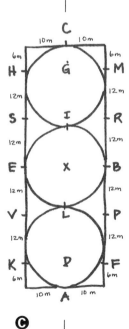

Ⓒ

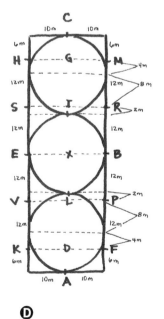

Ⓓ

stride or two in canter before you ask for the walk. Since he doesn't want to walk forward, supple and ride him a few strides sideways before asking for the new lead. Think of having a little "renvers-left feeling" before you ask for the new lead, as well. This will help keep him connected to the outside (right) rein and hopefully keep him in a better contact.

....

Q Can you offer any help with the timing of the aids for the two-tempis?

A See my answer to the next question about one-tempi changes.

....

Q I have a question about the one-tempi changes. I am new at them, preparing for Intermediare 2. I have the three-tempis down nicely. Getting the two-tempis is difficult! I get excited, then get too busy, and of course, that confuses the issue!

A The two-tempis and the one-tempis can have similar problems. They are basically a series of good, single changes. So there are a few tests each day to work on before you start into them. First, make sure you have a good quality canter with the ability to ride the horse very straight on the quarterline. I also think some simple changes to test this straightness and the new aid for the canter departs should be practiced. Remember, the horse needs to have a quick reaction to the canter-depart aid. Once you have done your homework, do a few one-tempis on the quarterline to help you think about your straightness. If you feel you have to force the aid, or throw yourself or your horse around to

get it done, then you need to go back and do your homework!

In these series, horses lose their straightness, then also the impulsion, and it is too difficult for them to continue. Don't be afraid to ride a little more forward in the canter prior to starting the changes, and also don't be afraid to stop asking for the changes when the canter quality falls apart. Just go forward a bit and refresh the canter.

....

Q When leg-yielding, I always have too much bend through the body and cause my horse to "pop" his outside shoulder. I see a lot of riders making the same mistake. Any advice?

A The leg-yield is the second lateral movement we teach the horse. The correct use of leg-yield will teach the horse to move more off the inside leg and over to the outside rein. However, a lot of horses figure out quickly they can move their weight onto the outside shoulder rather than really increasing the lateral suppleness of their body. I suggest you go back to turn-on-the-forehand for a while and teach the horse to keep his outside shoulder more in place with the outside rein and a small amount of counterflexion as you move the hindquarters over. Some work in hand will help with the correct reaction to this aid, too. Then, when you do your leg-yields, don't be afraid to counterflex the horse a bit at times to remind him not to push through the shoulders.

Q I used to ride with hunter/jumper trainers and many were critical of the demands put on dressage horses, saying that at the highest levels many of the movements are unnatural. This seems contradictory to what dressage is about: willingness and fluidity. Comments please?

A I would just point out that our dressage athletes are often 17 years old at the Olympic Games and still sound. Good dressage improves the horse's physique and, therefore, his longevity. I often see "dressage movements" from foals in the pasture. The only thing I don't see is a horse doing half-pass or going sideways.

Q I was hoping to get some insight on a problem that I have been having with my mare. She is a nine-year-old Danish Warmblood—lightly under saddle, mostly walk and trot. She is really stiff to the left. We have been working on lots of bending and suppling that direction. Figure eights help. Lately, she has been "fishtailing" when I ask her to bend left: she swings her butt way out! I try to use my outside leg but she stops dead and will throw her head all around. I try to reinforce with a whip but that makes her buck. I am stuck on trying how to fix this.

A Make sure you go back to see if your mare really understands all the bending aids. It sounds as if she understands the inside rein to bend the neck and turn the shoulders, and also to move her rib cage away from the inside leg. I am not so certain she understands that the outside leg behind the girth means to keep the haunches in. I would work a bit at walk with head-to-the-wall leg-yield, and introduce—or reintroduce—the response to the outside leg behind the girth.

Q How should a rider know if she is ready to show a certain level?

A Good question! I think that people say, "I am a Third Level rider," or "My horse is at Third Level," just because the horse does a flying change. They don't realize that the other piece is the horse's balance: the horse might do flying-changes or even a half-pass, but does the horse perform with collection and cadence? Is the horse uphill? Are the basics

AHA! Moment

My "Aha!" moment was when I figured out how to use the dressage movements to train my horse—not just to train my horse to do the movements!

Janet says: The movements are there to help us create suppleness, collection, and engagement. However, the movements can be dangerous without good basics: for example, I see horses that love to go sideways, but the riders cannot ride them on a straight line! This is an incorrect use of lateral work. Also, remember you need to be able to go more sideways or less sideways; in other words, be adjustable and in charge.

correct? I often say if the basics are correct, the movements will take care of themselves.

So the correct balance of the horse and the fulfillment of the Training Pyramid (which can be found on the front cover of every USEF Dressage Test under "Purpose") is of the utmost importance!

Q **I'm confused about what makes a "correct" half-halt.**

A There are actually different half-halts for different movements. The weighting of your seat, which leg is active, will tell the horse which movement to expect. The rebalancing half-halt is the perfect combination of the driving aids, the bending aids, and the outside rein.

CHAPTER TWELVE

Showing

Showing can be fun, or it can be a nerve-wracking experience. I don't believe that everyone *must* show; in fact, I have many students who love the training process and want to keep their money directed there, rather than the show ring. Other students just love it!

If you don't have a regular trainer, and lessons are hard to come by, showing will help you know where you are in the training process. Going to a schooling show can be very helpful, too, but I would suggest you make sure the judges have at least earned their "L" accreditation from USDF. This will tell you the judges have successfully shown, as well as gone through a very good educational program and taken an exam. Going to a show is about getting good feedback, not about getting a ribbon. So, whether you go to a schooling show or a USEF/USDF recognized show, be sure you check out the list of judges and their credentials.

If you are the type of person who is too nervous to show, volunteer to help groom for your friends and be sure to watch their rides and ask to read their tests. Organizing a "fun" show at your barn where a good friend who is an "L" graduate comes and judges might also help you get over your nerves. Remember, you can still be a great dressage rider without the show ring. If you don't want to show, don't be pressured into it!

GUIDELINES

For those of you who love to show, let me warn you not to wear your horse out. It is sad that USEF had to put a rule in place in order to stop dressage riders from entering too many classes each day.

If your horse is high energy, two national tests a day is fine. Three, in my opinion, is not a good idea, even though allowed in the rules. Remember, at home, you only ride once a day, and that, plus your warm up and a lesson, perhaps, is no more than an hour. When doing national classes, you will have three 30-minute warm ups and three classes of 10 minutes. That is two hours of riding, double what your horse is used to doing each day. For the FEI Levels, in national shows, two tests are allowed, but in CDI events, only one test is permitted. Be fair to your horse and he will enjoy showing, as well.

Be sure to take into account the journey. Long periods of time in the trailer will create some stiffness in your horse, which you might see for one or two days after the trip. Don't expect to unload and jump on your horse for a long schooling session. Arrive early and plan a day to just walk around the show grounds and let him see the sights and relax.

Test Tips

- Rider fitness and preparation should be addressed. Make sure you can ride two tests per day effectively and not wear out. Practice your tests at home so you know the patterns—even when you have a reader. Inaccuracy and cutting corners is the most common way riders lose points. There are so many things at a show you don't have control over so don't throw points away foolishly!

- Be sure to check that your show clothes fit you and look neat and professional. Take your coat to a tailor and have it fitted properly. There are too many incorrectly fitting jackets in the show ring. Gloves are a must, white or black. Clean saddle pads, one for each day, please. Do not polish the inside of your boots as this will rub off on your horse and the pad. Have a friend there before you go into the ring to check all of your keepers on the bridle and girth. Dust off your boots with a damp cloth.

- Remember your ride time of 10:00 a.m. means you are *going down the centerline* at 10:00 a.m. Check with the ring steward when you first arrive in the warm-up area. Find out if that ring is on time. Ask for the horse's number right before your ride, then identify that horse in the warm-up area. When that horse goes into the ring, get ready and put your coat on. As soon as the horse in front of you halts at the end of the test, enter the outside of the ring and familiarize your horse with the surroundings. First, go by the judges' stand and give the scribe your number. Keep this conversation to a minimum. Show the horse the judges' stand from both directions and then proceed down to the "A" end. Remember, after the bell you have 45 seconds. This is not enough time to go all the way around the ring again.

- Your reader must be at the ring at the start of your test and begin reading immediately after the bell. You can be eliminated if your reader shows up late and starts reading after you are already in the ring.

- Know the test "boxes" well enough so that if there is a mistake or a spook, you can try to keep the low score limited to one box. Don't punish your horse in the ring. If he has made a mistake, move on: the low score will not go up if you try to fix it, and it might make things worse!

- At the end of the day, read your tests, talk to your trainer and discuss where you can improve your performance the next day. Judges appreciate riders who show that they have read their comments.

• STORY FROM THE ROAD •

MOST OF THEM, LOVELY EXPERIENCES...

When I was a new judge, I had not learned that you always asked for the hotel address so that in case you are left in the lurch, you can take a taxi. I waited at the airport for three hours until finally giving up and walking across the street to the airport hotel to book a room. The next morning I returned to wait curbside at the airport, figuring at some point the show staff would realize there was not a judge in the booth or the hotel they'd booked for me. I finally did get picked up, and the show started a bit late. By the way, I never went back to that show location again.

Another time, two of us had flights that were delayed, and we were picked up and left at the front door of the hotel around 2:00 a.m. No one came in with us. Since no one from the show had called the hotel and guaranteed us for late arrival, our rooms had been given away. We slept in the lobby the first night.

Another show was located between two airports (which I did not know) and while the management picked me up at the correct airport, the volunteer who took me back to the airport when the show was over did not ask which one, and I was not familiar with the area. He took me to the wrong airport, and by the time we figured it out, it was too late to backtrack.

I think every judge has stories of food poisoning, bed bugs, missed pickups, and glitches. But at the end of the day, after 35 years, most of the experiences have been lovely, and I have fully enjoyed meeting new people, seeing new venues and having had an expense-paid journey all around the United States. There are many, many places I look forward to going back to every few years, and many show managers and GMO groups I love to work for and with.

~ PROBLEMS ~
and Solutions

Q **How does music help dressage riding?**

A For maintaining a steady tempo in the trot, riding to music is especially helpful. If you have a horse that is a bit slow, pick music with a quicker tempo than the horse likes! For a horse that likes to run away a bit, pick something a bit mellower, with a slower tempo. It can help to ride with a metronome attached to your belt: set it to the correct tempo you are trying to achieve.

. . . .

Q **What are your feelings about schooling shows? Do you recommend them for young horses and new riders, or is it better to be in a recognized show with enforced rules and recognized judges?**

A There are schooling shows that have "L" Graduates as judges, which I recommend. I would not go to a show with Aunt Sally from down the road judging because you want an educated judge to look at your ride and give you a good evaluation that includes comments and scores that will be mirrored at a recognized show.

Here are some things to look for at *schooling* and *recognized* shows:

Schooling Show

- A safe arena with good footing. Be aware, "chain" encircled arenas are not allowed at recognized shows for safety reasons.
- Another safe area (also with good footing) to longe your horse.
- Decent stabling in case your horse doesn't tie well to the trailer.
- A judge that is an "L" Graduate.

- A quiet atmosphere. (Sometimes, there is just too much going on around the arena at a schooling show.)

Recognized Show

- Good footing in all arenas and warm-up areas.
- A well-respected judge.
- Safe stabling.
- A good longeing area.
- Arenas that are not over-decorated or have judge's boxes that spook the horses! Note: Usually a Level 2 show will fulfill these requirements without all the hoopla a Level 3 or 4 show requires!

I think schooling shows are fine when they are well run. My concern is with a young horse—nervous to begin with—being surrounded by inexperienced riders and horses; they might not give your horse a comfortable experience. And, the rules (basically none that can be enforced) are hit and miss. Be smart and know what you are getting yourself into.

. . . .

Q **How do you mentally get ready for a show, beat the jitters, and make it like it's just another practice? Or, do you do even that? I personally need a mental pre-show mantra or something!**

A Well, I have to say with over 30 years of showing, I've always had a little case of the nerves—going to the loo, smoking a "ciggie" (when I did that bad thing!) I don't think being a little nervous is a bad thing. The best way to overcome nerves that can destroy your performance is to be really prepared.

You will need to memorize your test, even if you have a caller. You will need to have practiced *all* the movements and know exactly how to ride the figures accurately. You should not overface your horse: I strongly recommend you show a level below where you are training. You should not attempt a movement you cannot perform 90 percent of the time at home in training.

I also have my students take a copy of the dressage test and write in the comment box what they are going to be thinking for the movement. For example, for entering the arena, they write: *Enter on the left rein (because the horse is easier to straighten that way) three strides before X, start to half-halt to shorten the trot (or the canter), and put more weight on the hind legs. Halt. Breathe out. Salute, but don't take your eyes off the judge. Do not adjust your seat or legs (as the horse will become crooked). Move off, near G bend in the direction of the turn, and use the first corner!*

This gets the riders thinking about each step of each movement: where to bend, where to collect, and where to check the straightness. It keeps their minds busy, instead of being nervous.

Q What is the best strategy for warming up different types of horses?

A Good question. There is an in-depth chapter on this in *Dressage for the Not-So-Perfect Horse*. However, for now I'd say that basically, if you have a tense horse, you will need to design a warm-up that will relax his body and his mind. Lots of circles and curved lines are very beneficial, and bending stretches his muscles, which helps him to relax. "Stretchy circles" are also useful if the horse will allow this at the beginning: some tense horses won't. Be a bit boring with this type of horse!

For the lazy guy, do lots of transitions and work to make him quicker off the aids to help him "wake up." Boring this one would only make things worse! Make the work interesting and keep asking for quick responses to your questions.

To summarize: A *nervous* horse takes more time. Do lots of walking on a long rein, perhaps even an early-morning workout prior to the scheduled class warm-up. The *lazy* horse won't need as much time, but concentrate on making him sharp to the aids. Of course, you will have to think about the weather too. Too hot? Do less. Cold? Do more. A horse that tends to fall apart and get "long" should not be warmed up with a lot of stretching, whereas the tight, tense horse needs just that! I try to keep it simple: note the horse's behavior that day and try to change it in the warm-up.

Q What is a good way to find out which bloodlines are best for dressage?

A Of course, the Europeans are way ahead of us in tracking performance standards for their bloodlines. You can look at any studbook and see the quality and scores for the horse's gaits, rideability, and at which discipline he or she excels! These are great statistics to check out. I know when I first started buying horses in Europe, I didn't know about these facts and bought a few horses that were wonderful movers but did not have the mind for dressage training. The USEF and USDF are now keeping track of bloodlines, so there is a lot more information around. Do your research, ask questions from the many knowledgeable people in the United States, then you can feel you are starting with the best "raw product" you can buy!

Q Why has "competitive dressage" strayed so far from "classical dressage"?

A I gave this question a lot of thought and talked to quite a few people, too. In riding facilities where there has been a lot of education, this is not true. However, without the type of schools and programs they have in Europe, anyone in the United States can hang out a shingle and become a trainer. It takes years to learn this sport, and having competed a horse trained by someone else, even if successfully, does not a trainer make. A rider, perhaps, but not a trainer. A trainer is someone who knows the step-by-step process of educating the horse in the proper way.

Originally, classically schooled horses were developed for use in battle. On Baroque breeds, with easier gaits to ride, riders' lives depended on the horses responding to the aids. When machines took over the horse's role in war, dressage was turned into a sport. The classical school dealt mostly with collection and collecting movements, like the airs above the ground, which are still performed in all European classical schools. The gaits of the horse were not so important and extensions were just not part of the training. What soldier would want to ride the new elastic and huge trots found in modern competition? Now, the quality of the training and improvement of the gaits are of utmost importance. The gaits must be elastic, and all of the expression and impulsion come from the horse's ability to use his back.

Q I loved the short stories you shared in your first book about some of the horses you've ridden. It's fun to hear about how they progressed over time, and it's helpful to hear about the difficult horses, too. When we see the finished product in the show ring, it's easy to forget that the road getting there might have been bumpy, even for trainers we think highly of! Can you share another?

A One of my favorite stories is about a Holsteiner gelding I owned named Halloh. I bought him as a five-year-old in Germany; he was a lovely horse and moved beautifully but a bit difficult in the mind, at times. By the time I bought him I had quite a bit of experience training horses to the FEI Levels, but wanted a really good Grand Prix horse. I had decided that taking the time out to show really slowed the training down too much. I had plenty of other client horses to show, so full-time training with no showing was on the horizon for Halloh.

I finally took him to his first show—at Prix St. Georges—in Sun Valley, Idaho, at River Grove Farms (home of Brentina, Olympian Debbie McDonald's wonderful mare). It was a beautiful farm with a trout stream flowing through the middle. Hilda Gurney was the judge. Well, there was a big, blue-plastic-covered, fiberglass longe ring not too far from the main show ring. It was just my luck that a horse was in there when I entered at A, and the noise from the sand being thrown up against the plastic walls sent Halloh into a tizzy. (Take a tip from me—sand on plastic can be an issue! See my story about Electus on page 104.) I did two movements and then "left" the area. Hilda invited me back in, and I performed two more movements before I exited again. Hilda finally left the box and gave me a short lecture about our performance.

I obviously should have given him more experiences in the "real world" before the show, so with my tail firmly between my legs, I took Halloh to check out that longe ring that afternoon and also the next morning before his class. The good news was that we stayed in the arena and won our class! The bad news was he was a bit tired so we were not as brilliant as I hoped.

I also had a Holsteiner mare named Malene, and I was riding her in a First Level test in Longmont when a huge Colorado thunderstorm came up: hail, wind, and lightning. Just as we galloped down the long side for our canter lengthening, the flowerpot at B fell into the ring. Malene jumped right over it and continued on her way. I was a bit upset that I only received a "4" on this movement and that the judge did not allow for the weather conditions.

Q Why are sleeveless shirts not allowed when coats are deemed optional?

A Good question, and I really don't know the reason. I was on the Dressage Committee for over 16 years and this rule was already in place, so I was never "in" on the discussion. I think it probably has to do with looks: shirts with sleeves look a bit "dressier" than ones without.

Q How fast should we be pushing our horses up the levels? It seems if we are not keeping up with the track of the Europeans we are behind. What is right?

A It depends on the talent of the horse and the ability of the rider. A really top young horse can move more quickly up the levels, as in the young horse program, where a six-year-old is doing flying changes, and a seven-year-old is ready for a Green Prix St. Georges, and a nine-year-old is ready for a Green Grand Prix. I've had only two of these horses in my career, so they don't grow on trees!

Q I am bothered by the fact that I constantly hear from riders in other disciplines that dressage is boring. Why do people who don't ride dressage think we are boring?

A Boring? Maybe, for some. For me, the sport is fascinating. But I do think you need to have a certain type of personality to love dressage. Many of my friends were more adrenaline junkies. They loved eventing and still do it today. I did it in my late twenties because I was part of that group, but I did not enjoy the cross-country. I don't even like riding on a Ferris wheel! So, jumping and running at high speed was never my idea of fun. I often say that "dressage" is French for "afraid to jump"!

I do have the type of personality that enjoys discovering things. I love mystery novels and TV detective shows. Dressage is like a detective novel: I need to discover every day where my horse is avoiding work, where he is stiff, which aid he is not reacting correctly to. This process fascinates me.

Q **Are you seeing more horses going barefoot in the show arena?**

A To be honest, unless a horse throws a shoe *in* the ring, this is something I don't notice. Most of the arenas where I judge are well watered, so the footing always sticks a bit to the horse's foot and hides the shoe anyway.

Q **When showing at the lower levels, what bit can be used when the snaffle does not work?**

A The snaffle is what you *must* use according to the rules. Why doesn't a snaffle "work"? Does your horse run away? Will your horse not go "on the bit?" I would caution you to not just blame the issue on the horse's mouth. Most problems start *behind* the mouth, and he might be stiff in his back or neck, and you just see the result of that in the hand. I would suggest you go to a trainer with a good background with young or green horses and have your horse evaluated rather than just getting a sharper bit. I would also suggest you ask your vet to check his teeth, as he may be in pain.

Q **In regard to riding a test at a show and entering at A, is the start of the centerline located directly in front of A when A is placed to the left or right of the middle of the opening, or does the centerline start in the center of the opening regardless of where A is placed?**

A First, if you are at a recognized show, the Technical Delegate should have placed A in the correct spot during the ring check. A should be in line with C, and far enough outside and back so that the rider has no problem entering the arena. However, if for some reason (maybe during the ring being dragged?) A has been moved off center, you need to ignore its position and remember that A should be lined up directly opposite C.

Q **I really enjoy riding in a bitless bridle. I don't understand why it is not allowed in dressage competition. I know that a horse can be collected and show all the desired dressage attributes without any tack at all. So why the restriction?**

A The USEF Dressage Committee has addressed this subject several times. I have ridden in a bitless bridle, as well, and found it very useful on some horses, but not on all. In The Netherlands it is allowed in dressage competition at the lower levels. I think in the United States we are still following the FEI Guidelines for the most part and do not venture too far away from them. I am sure there will be more discussion about this, and perhaps at some point, it will be legal for the lower national levels here.

Q My little Arab mare has never liked any of the snaffle bits I've tried. A clinician told me that my bits were way too bulky for her tiny mouth, and I should try the skinniest bit I could find. This bit ended up being a thin bradoon from a 40-year-old bridle! My mare loves it! She even opens her mouth to take it when I bridle her. Can I show in this bit?

A I often tell students that their bits are too small, big, short, or long for their horse! It is important to use the type of bit that fits comfortably: the size of the horse's mouth and tongue are very important when determining this fit! Snaffles are permitted in dressage in all of the levels now, up through Grand Prix. The rules on what is legal or not change a bit from year to year. The best thing for you to do is to go to the USEF website and download the photos of legal snaffles. The mouthpieces and the rings can go together in any fashion.

Q Just when I thought I was figuring out the dressage system, my daughter gets a score that shocks me! Why does it seem that judges are consistent with their comments while inconsistent with their number scores?

A Well, as a judge trainer, I am pleased that you tell me that comments are consistent! In our forums, we are always stressing good and helpful comments, and of course, we try to standardize the scores as well. Sometimes, I find that judges with less experience will score lower than FEI judges. They are still too intent at seeing all the little details. FEI judges look at the big picture first, and then notice the small details. Sometimes, there is only a difference of one point. I might give a 6.5 or 7, thinking the movement was "fairly good," and the other judge a 5.5 or 6, thinking it was only "satisfactory." At the end of the test, if every box had a one-point spread, the total score could be quite different.

Also, as in the real world in any job, there are excellent judges who go to judges' forums even when they are not required, and there are others who only do the bare minimum and sit in the back of the room.

• STORY FROM THE ROAD •

ROAD WARRIOR

Driving horses all over the United States in all kinds of weather can be tricky. I went every year either East or West for the Regional Championships and to train. There were only three Regionals in those days, East, West and one in the middle. A couple of times, they were in Colorado (I arranged both of those and the management team was made up of horse husbands!) Once I went to Chicago, Illinois, and once to Waco, Texas, but usually, I ended up in California, either in Los Angeles or Sacramento.

The same judges were flown around to these shows on three consecutive weekends. At one Regionals in Pebble Beach, California, I not only competed two horses, I took my judges' exam for my "R" rating (not allowed today). The time of year was usually September, and after I stayed and took lessons for a few weeks, I would be back on the road home to Colorado around the beginning of October.

Three times I met weather problems and closed roads. Luckily, the first time, I only had two horses. A blizzard hit Donner Pass and the road was closed. I was very lucky that a state patrol told me about a barn that was not too far away. We found a place for the horses and then had to trek all the way back to Sacramento for a hotel room. The next day the roads were cleared and we were back on the road.

Another time I was near Little America in Wyoming. Roads became a total skating rink and were all closed. There was nothing for miles except for this truck stop, so with four horses and my groom, we settled in for the night. The horses drank well and ate nets full of hay. My groom and I enjoyed the chatter from our CB Radio that night. My "handle" was Pony Express. Seems to be a lot of action at these truck stops!

One trip was quite scary. It was snowing; we were in Wyoming with four horses and my groom. We had two stallions and two geldings. The electrical system went out on my truck, so no wipers and no headlights. We found a county fairgrounds and were given stalls for the horses—not in a horse barn but a sheep barn. I took one look at the low sheep stalls and thought, "Oh dear, who will be alive tomorrow?"

My groom and I went to a hotel with no heat, and we *froze*. Early the next morning we held our breath as we opened the barn door…and everyone had been a good boy. I think the horses were just too tired to get into trouble! We loaded up and made it home.

I have had students who had trailer brakes burn out in the mountains, and one who had her hitch come loose on the way to Chicago…and the trailer actually left the truck! Thank goodness all these stories over the years had happy endings! I was truly blessed.

FINAL THOUGHTS

I hope that this book answered some of the questions you may have had at hand. I know that your questions will change as you become more educated and experienced in the sport of dressage.

Remember that each horse will teach you something. Sometimes, the horse will also teach you what *not* to do. Take these lessons in stride, and keep learning and questioning! With dressage we are never really a "finished" product! When you think you know it all, you will fail.

I look forward to meeting and talking to each and every one of you sometime in the future! May our paths cross soon. Until then, best wishes and happy riding!

Janet Foy

DRESSAGE FOR THE NOT-SO-PERFECT HORSE

RIDING THROUGH THE LEVELS
on the Peculiar, Opinionated, Complicated Mounts We All Love

JANET FOY
USEF S AND FEI 4* DRESSAGE JUDGE

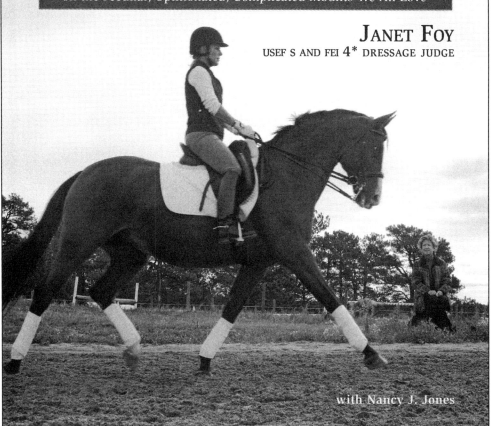

with Nancy J. Jones

INDEX